Knitted Toys

20 cute and colorful projects

Jody Long

Dover Publications, Inc.

Mineola, New York

This book is dedicated to:

My Nan Josephine Stenning, Pauline Bond,
and Linda O'Farrell for teaching me to knit.
I couldn't have done this without you three!

Bibliographical Note

Knitted Toys: 20 Cute and Colorful Projects is a new work, first published
by Dover Publications, Inc., in 2016.

Library of Congress Cataloging-in-Publication Data

Names: Long, Jody, 1984– author.
Title: Knitted toys : 20 cute and colorful projects / Jody Long.
Description: Mineola, New York : Dover Publications, 2016.
Identifiers: LCCN 2016017768 | ISBN 9780486802886 (paperback) | ISBN
    0486802884 (paperback)
Subjects: LCSH: Knitting—Patterns. | Soft toys. | BISAC: CRAFTS & HOBBIES /
    Needlework / Knitting. | CRAFTS & HOBBIES / Stuffed Animals.
Classification: LCC TT829 .L64 2016 | DDC 745.592/4—dc23 LC record
available at https://lccn.loc.gov/2016017768

Manufactured in the United States by RR Donnelley
80288401   2016
www.doverpublications.com

CONTENTS

INTRODUCTION

Knitted toys are the nicest kind of all, ideal for young children as they are soft, comforting, and washable. They are easy to make and fun to give, and will provide hours of playtime fun. Some parts of the toy can be knitted in the child's favorite colors. Each toy has its own personal character and by changing facial expressions or colors, new characters will develop, giving a never-ending list of things to make. All of the toys featured in this book are made from double knitting yarn and require 3.5oz/100g of any one color or less.

Toy Safety

All toys should be stuffed with nonflammable, washable stuffing. Always make sure that the toy is safe for the child who will receive it. Remember that very small toys are not suitable for babies and toddlers, because they could present a choking hazard.

Children under three years of age should not be given any toy that has small pieces which may be easily swallowed. When making toys, ensure that all pieces are securely sewn together and fastened firmly in place as instructed.

Never use buttons for eyes or decorations as they can easily come loose. Always embroider the faces and details as described in the instructions. A few of the toys in this book also use plastic drinking straws for strengthening parts; never be tempted to use pipe cleaners as these have sharp wire inside of the chenille coating. Some of the toys use cardboard in order to shape or flatten the toy/accessory; therefore these toys are not washable. If you prefer a toy that is fully washable, then make up the pattern as given and replace the cardboard with toy stuffing.

Choosing Yarn

Always use machine washable yarn as this generally keeps its shape and color well. Bear in mind that because toys are well loved and played with, they get dirty very quickly and may need frequent washings. Acrylic yarns are recommended because they are reasonably priced, machine washable, keep their color well, and come in a huge range of attractive shades.

If you are going to make several toys, the larger balls of yarn generally work out cheaper. Always check your tension when starting a toy and should you use more than one brand of yarn, check the tension on the new brand.

Yarn Information

Stylecraft Special Double Knit 3.5oz/100g ball, 100% Premium Acrylic, 322y/295m.

What if I can't find Stylecraft Yarns at my local yarn store?

The great thing about using acrylic yarns is most major yarn manufacturers make their own lines of acrylic, so if Stylecraft cannot be found, many alternatives are available within the market. You may wish to seek advice from your local yarn store, or read the "How to Substitute a Yarn" section below. Some alternative acrylic yarns are Lion Brand, Red Heart, or Plymouth Yarn.

How to Substitute a Yarn

Throughout this book, Stylecraft Special Double Knitting was used, which has a weight of 3.5oz/100g per ball, and a yardage of 322/295m. It is extremely simple to find a substitute yarn by using this simple equation. If the toy you're going to knit takes 3.5oz/100g of yarn in Stylecraft Special Double Knitting, which has the yardage of 322/295m, and your new substitute yarn has a yardage of 197/180m, you will need to divide the recommended yarn yardage 322 by the new yarn of 197 = 1.63 balls. As you can't buy part balls, you will need to buy two balls of the new substitute yarn to obtain the amount needed for your toy. I recommend always substituting with the same or similar weight yarn to avoid problems.

Amount of Yarn

The main color of any toy can be made from 3.5oz/100g of yarn or less, and oddments can be used for the other parts in some cases. Yarn amounts specified in the patterns can never be absolutely correct. This is partly due to the fact that tensions vary according to the knitter, but mostly because the number of yards/meters per ounce/gram varies with every color of yarn. To ensure that you will not run out of yarn, the yarn amounts given in the patterns are generous.

Equipment

Pins: Always use large glass/plastic-headed pins so they cannot pass through the knitted stitches and become lost within the stuffing, which would make the toy extremely dangerous.

Sewing needle: Always use a wool (knitter's) sewing needle for sewing up as these tend to be blunt and will not split the yarn fiber or stitches, resulting in a neater seam.

Tweezers: Can be extremely helpful when it comes to turning tiny pieces the right way and placing toy stuffing in awkward, hard-to-reach places.

Stitch holders: These prevent stitches from unraveling when not in use. Alternately, a spare knitting needle of the same size or less (ideally double pointed) can be used as a stitch holder. For holding just a few stitches, a safety pin is always useful.

Adhesive: Only use nontoxic, clear drying glue.

Gauge

It is important to check your tension before you start knitting. Knit a swatch using the specified yarn and knitting needles. If there are too many stitches to 4in/10cm, your tension is tight and you should change to a larger-sized needle. If there are too few stitches, your tension is loose and you should change to a smaller-sized needle.

Casting On (Cable Method)

Although there are many different techniques for casting on stitches, the following method creates a firm and attractive edge:

First make a slip knot in the yarn and place the loop on the left-hand needle. Insert the point of the right-hand needle into the loop on the left-hand needle, wind the yarn around the right-hand needle and draw the yarn through the loop. Pass the new loop onto the left-hand needle and pull the yarn to tighten the new loop.

Next insert the right-hand needle between the two loops on the left-hand needle, wind the yarn round the right-hand needle and draw the yarn through. Slip the new loop onto the left-hand needle as before.

Continue in this way, inserting the needle between two loops on the left-hand needle, until you have the required number of stitches.

Basic Stitches

Here is how to work the simple stitches used for the toys:

Stockinette Stitch: Alternate one row knit and one row purl. The knit side is the right side of the work unless otherwise stated in the instructions.

Garter Stitch: Knit every row. Both sides are the same and look identical.

K1, P1 Rib: Alternate one knit stitch with one purl stitch to the end of the row. On the next row, knit all the knit stitches and purl all the purl stitches as they face you.

Seed Stitch: Alternate one knit stitch with one purl stitch to the end of the row. On the next row, knit all the purl stitches and purl all the knit stitches as they face you.

Joining Yarn
Always join yarn at the beginning of a new row (unless you're working the Fair Isle or Intarsia Method), and never knot the yarn as the knot may come through to the right side and spoil your work. Any long loose ends will be useful for sewing up afterwards.

Working Stripes
When knitting different-colored stripes, carry yarns loosely up the side of your work.

Fair Isle Method
When two or three colors are worked repeatedly across a row, strand the yarn not in use loosely behind the stitches being worked. Always spread the stitches to their correct width to keep them elastic. It is advisable not to carry the stranded or "floating" yarns over more than three stitches at a time, but to weave them under and over the color you are working. The "floating" yarns are therefore caught at the back of the work.

Intarsia Method
The simplest way to do this is to cut short lengths of yarn for each motif or block of color used in a row. Then joining in the various colors at the appropriate point on the row, link one color to the next by twisting them around each other where they meet on the wrong side of work to avoid gaps. All ends can then either be darned along the color join lines, as each motif is completed, or they can be "knitted-in" to the fabric of the knitting as each color is worked into the pattern. This is done in much the same way as "weaving-in" yarns when working the Fair Isle method and does save time darning-in ends.

Working from a Chart
Each square on a chart represents a stitch and each line of squares a row of knitting. Alongside the chart there will be a color key. When working from the charts, read odd rows (knit) from right to left and even rows (purl) from left to right, unless otherwise stated.

Seams
There is no need to press the knitted pieces of the toys prior to sewing up. I recommend mattress stitch as this saves turning tiny parts right side out. It also helps matching row for row and stripe for stripe on knitted fabric. If you are unable to mattress stitch, then a simple backstitch will be fine. Whichever method you choose for sewing your toy together, a one stitch seam allowance has been given on all pieces.

Finishing
The finishing instructions are displayed below each piece, so you can make them up as you go along so you are not left with a confusing heap of pieces at the end. Studying the pictures of the toy will give you the best guide to the finishing touches.

Stuffing
To save a toy from going lumpy you must tear small pieces of stuffing apart and tease the edges out, as these teased parts form together when placing more stuffing into the toy and gives a much better result. While you need to stuff your toy firmly to withstand the

endless hours of play, never overstuff as this will result in seeing the stuffing through the knitted stitches; understuffing, however, will lead to a floppy toy.

Coloring Cheeks
Slightly dampen the end of a red-colored pencil in water; rub the side of the point gently in a circular motion against the knitted fabric until the desired size and depth of red is achieved. Never use paint pencils as this type will color run in the wash.

Embroidered Stitches
To work any embroidered stitches on a stuffed toy, it is sometimes necessary to start and finish off the yarn ends invisibly. If this is required, proceed as follows:

Thread a blunt-ended wool needle with yarn required and knot end of yarn. Take needle through the stuffed toy part, passing between the knitted stitches, and bring it out at the position required. Pull the yarn to draw the knotted end right inside the stuffing. Tug the yarn to make sure the knot is caught in the stuffing.

Now work the required embroidered stitches. Pass the needle back through the knitted part to come out at a position between the knitted stitches. Pass needle back through knitted part again between the same knitted stitches to come out at a different position. Repeat until yarn is securely fastened off, then pull end of yarn and snip off close to the knitted stitches.

Occasional Rows Worked in Double Yarn
There are occasions in the instructions where one or more rows are worked using two strands of yarn together, changing back to a single strand of yarn for subsequent rows. When changing from double to single yarn, treat the two loops on each stitch on the previous row as one stitch when working the next row.

Instructions in Square Brackets
These are to be repeated the number of times stated after the closing bracket.

Binding Off
Always bind off k-wise unless otherwise stated.

Working in Stockinette Stitch
Always begin with a K row unless otherwise stated.

NEEDLE CONVERSION
US—UK GLOSSARY

US	UK
0	2.00
1	2.25
–	2.50
2	2.75
2	3.00
3	3.25
4	3.50
5	3.75
6	4.00
7	4.50
8	5.00
9	5.50
10	6.00
10.5	6.50
–	7.00
–	7.50
11	8.00
13	9.00
15	10.00
Seed St	Moss St
Stockinette St	Stocking St
Bind off	Cast off
Gauge	Tension

ABBREVIATIONS

alt	alternate
beg	begin/beginning
bet	between
BO	bind off
cm	centimeter(s)
CO	cast on
cont	continue
dec	decrease/decreases/decreasing
dpn	double pointed needle(s)
foll	follow/follows/following
g	gram(s)
Gst	garter stitch
in	inch(es)
inc	increase/increases/increasing
K	knit
Kfb	knit into front and back of next st
k-wise	knit-wise
m	marker
mm	millimeter(s)
oz	ounce(s)
P	purl
patt	pattern(s)
pm	place marker
psso	pass slipped stitch over
p-wise	purl-wise
rem	remain/remaining
rep	repeat(s)
Rev St st	reverse stockinette stitch
RS	right side
skp	slip 1, K1, pass slip st over
sl	slip
sl st	slip stitch(es)
St st	stockinette stitch
st(s)	stitch(es)
tbl	through back loop
tog	together
WS	wrong side
y	yarn
yb	yarn to back
yf	yarn to front
yo	yarn over

Artie the Airplane

Measurements

Length: 11in/28cm, Wingspan: 16in/40cm

Materials

* Stylecraft Special DK 3.5oz/100g balls 100% Acrylic, one ball each:
  Aster 1003 (A), Matador 1010 (B), Sunshine 1114 (C), Silver 1203 (D), and
  Black 1002 (E)
* 2.8oz/80g Stuffing
* One 5mm plastic drinking straw
* 4mm thick cardboard
* Pins
* US 2 (3mm) Knitting needles

Gauge

26 sts and 36 rows = 4in/10cm in St st.

BODY

With A, beg at tail, CO 10.

Rows 1–2, 4–8, 10–24, 26–40, 42–56, 58–72, 74–88, 90–92: St st.
Row 3: Kfb in each st across—20 sts.
Row 9: [K1, Kfb, K2] across—25 sts.
Row 25: [K2, Kfb, K2] across—30 sts.
Row 41: [K2, Kfb, K3] across—35 sts.
Row 57: [K3, Kfb, K3] across—40 sts.
Row 73: [K3, Kfb, K4] across—45 sts.
Row 89: [K4, Kfb, K4] across—50 sts.

NOSE

Row 93: [K3, K2tog] across—40 sts.
Rows 94, 96, 98: P.
Row 95: [K2, K2tog] across—30 sts.
Row 97: [K1, K2tog] across—20 sts.
Row 99: K2tog across—10 sts.

Cut yarn leaving a long tail, thread tail through rem sts, gather tightly and fasten off. Sew ends of rows tog creating a seam underneath body, stuffing body firmly before closing seam. Tightly gather CO edge and fasten off.

NOSE CAP

With B, CO 20.

Row 1–2, 4, 6: St st.
Row 3: [K1, K2tog, K1] across—15 sts.
Row 5: [K1, K2tog] across—10 sts.
Row 7: [K2tog] across—5 sts.

Cut yarn leaving a long tail, thread tail through rem sts, gather tightly and fasten off. Sew ends of rows tog and stuff firmly. With seam facing down, sew CO edge to front of airplane as illustrated.

PROPELLERS (make 3)

With C, CO 6.

Rows 1–2, 4–20: St st.
Row 3: Kfb across—12 sts.
Row 21: K2tog across—6 sts.

Cut yarn leaving a long tail, thread tail through rem sts, gather tightly and fasten off. Sew ends of rows tog for each propeller. Do not stuff. Tightly gather CO edge, and sew to nose cap, spacing propeller blades evenly around.

FRONT WINGS (make 2)

With A, CO 28.

Rows 1–2: St st.
Row 3: [K1, Kfb, K2] across—35 sts.

Cont in St st working stripe pattern as follows:

Rows 4–8, 19–48, 59–62: in A.
Rows 9–10, 17–18, 49–50, 57–58: in B.
Rows 11–16, 51–56: in C.

END OF WING

Row 63: [K1, K2tog, K2] across—28 sts.
Rows 64, 66, 68: P.
Row 65: [K1, K2tog, K1] across—21 sts.
Row 67: [K1, K2tog] across—14 sts.
Row 69: K2tog across—7 sts.

Cut yarn leaving a long tail, thread tail through rem sts, gather tightly and fasten off. Sew ends of rows tog. Cut strip of cardboard 2.75in/7cm x 7.5in/19cm. Round off the corners of one end to match the shaping at the end of each wing. Insert cardboard in wing. With seam along bottom of wing, sew wings on each side of body 1.5in/4cm from the nose shaping.

BACK WINGS (make 2)

With A, CO 21.

Rows 1–2, 4: St st.
Row 3: [K1, Kfb, K1] across—28 sts.

Cont in St st working stripe pattern as follows:

Rows 5–6, 11–12, 25–26, 31–32: in B.
Rows 7–10, 27–30: in C.
Rows 13–24, 33–34: in A.

END OF WING

Row 35: [K1, K2tog, K1] across—21 sts.
Rows 36, 38: P.
Row 37: [K1, K2tog] across—14 sts.
Row 39: K2tog across—7 sts.

Cut yarn leaving a long tail, thread tail through rem sts, gather tightly and fasten off. Sew ends of rows tog forming seam along bottom of each wing. Cut strip of cardboard 2.25in/6cm wide x 4.5in/11.5cm long out of 4mm-thick cardboard and round off the corners of one end to match the shaping of each wing. Insert cardboard in wing. Sew wings on each side of body 1.5in/4cm from beg of tail.

BACK TAIL FIN

With A, CO 20.

Rows 1, 3: K.
Row 2 and all WS rows: P.
Row 5: K8, k2tog, skp, K8—18 sts.
Row 7: Change to B, K7, K2tog, skp, K7—16 sts.
Row 9: Change to C, K6, K2tog, skp, K6—14 sts.
Row 11: Change to B, K5, K2tog, skp, K5—12 sts.
Row 13: Change to A, K4, K2tog, skp, K4—10 sts.
Row 15: K3, K2tog, skp, K3—8 sts.
Row 17: K2, K2tog, skp, K2—6 sts.
Row 19: K1, K2tog, skp, K1—4 sts.

Cut yarn leaving a long tail, thread tail through rem sts, gather tightly and fasten off. Sew ends of rows tog forming seam along back of fin. Cut a 1.5in/4cm x 2.25in/6cm strip of cardboard, shaping at front of fin. Insert the cardboard. Sew fin to center of body bet back wings.

LEGS (make 2)

With B, CO 5, work 18 rows in St st.

Cut yarn leaving a long tail, thread tail through rem sts, gather tightly and fasten off. Cut two 2in/5cm lengths of drinking straw. Sew ends of rows tog, insert the straw. Sew CO edge to underbody on either side of body seam and in line with front wing seams with 6 sts bet legs, making sure the legs can support the airplane.

WHEELS (make 2)

Using E, CO 5.

Row 1: Kfb in each st across—10 sts.
Rows 2–4: St st.
Rows 5–6: Change to D, St st.
Row 7: K2tog across—5 sts.

Cut yarn leaving a long tail, thread tail through rem sts, gather tightly and fasten off. With right side out, sew ends of rows tog. With D section facing outward, sew wheel to lower edge of leg.

FINISHING

Weave in all ends.

Buzzy the Bee

Measurements

17in/43cm x 12.5in/32cm

Materials

* Stylecraft Special DK 3.5oz/100g balls 100% Acrylic, one ball each: White 1001 (A), Sunshine 1114 (B), Black 1002 (C), Copper 1029 (D), Matador 1010 (E), Dark Brown 1004 (F), Meadow 1065 (G), Lipstick 1246 (H), and Turquoise 1068 (I)
* 5.25oz/150g Stuffing
* Stitch holder
* Stitch markers
* Knitting needles size US 2 (3mm) and US 6 (4mm)

Gauge

26 sts and 36 rows = 4in/10cm in St st using US 2 (3mm) needles.

NOTE: Use US 2 (3mm) needles throughout unless otherwise stated.

BODY

With C, beg at bottom, CO 12.

Row 1: K.
Row 2 and all WS rows: P.
Row 3: Kfb in each st across—24 sts.
Row 5: [Kfb, K1] across—36 sts.
Row 7: [K1, Kfb, K1] across—48 sts.
Row 9: [K1, Kfb, K2] across—60 sts.
Row 11: [K2, Kfb, K2] across—72 sts.
Row 13: [K2, Kfb, K3] across—84 sts.
Rows 15–54: In St st, work stripe pattern with 8 rows each of B and C.

Maintaining 8 row stripe patt, cont as follows:

Row 55: [K2, K2tog, K2] across—70 sts.
Rows 56–62, 64–70, 72–74: St st.
Row 63: [K1, K2tog, K2] across—56 sts.
Row 71: [K1, K2tog, K1] across—42 sts.

SHOULDERS

Row 75: K6, K2tog 5 times, K10, K2tog 5 times, K6—32 sts.
Rows 76–78: St st.

HEAD

Rows 79–80, 82: Cont with B only, St st.
Row 81: Kfb in each st across—64 sts.
Row 83: [K3, Kfb, K4] across—72 sts.
Rows 84–110: St st, pm in 2 center sts of rows 95 and 104.

TOP OF HEAD

Row 111: [K6, K2tog] across—63 sts.
Row 112 and all WS rows: P.
Row 113: [K5, K2tog] across—54 sts.
Row 115: [K4, K2tog] across—45 sts.
Row 117: [K3, K2tog] across—36 sts.
Row 119: [K2, K2tog] across—27 sts.
Row 121: [K1, K2tog] across—18 sts.
Row 122: P2tog across—9 sts.

Cut yarn leaving a long tail, thread tail through rem sts, gather tightly and fasten off. Tightly gather CO sts and fasten off. Sew ends of rows tog on body and head, stuffing body firmly before closing seam. With a length of B doubled, tightly gather first row of head, fasten off at back of neck.

NOSE

With B, embroider 3 sts over marked sts on row 95.

MOUTH

With C, embroider a "V" of two long stitches worked out from center, 6 rows below nose as pictured on page 6.

EYES (make 2)

With A, CO 12.

Row 1–4: St st.
Row 5: With C, K2tog across—6 sts.

Cut yarn leaving a long tail, thread tail through rem sts, gather tightly and fasten off. Tightly gather CO sts and fasten off. Sew ends of rows tog and stuff firmly. With I, embroider a circle of 8 chain sts around C on each eye. With A, make a tiny straight stitch for the twinkle of each eye. Sew eyes 3 sts from center at row 104 of head.

STINGER

With C, CO 12.

Rows 1–6, 8–10, 12–14, 16–20: St st.
Row 7: [K1, K2tog, K1] across—9 sts.
Row 11: [K1, K2tog] across—6 sts.
Row 15: K2tog across—3 sts.

Cut yarn leaving a long tail, thread tail through rem sts, gather tightly and fasten off. Sew ends of rows tog, stuff firmly and sew to base of body at back.

RIGHT LEG

With E, beg at sole of foot, CO 26.

Rows 1–2: St st.
Shape shoe point
Row 3: K11, K2tog, skp, K11—24 sts.
Row 4 and all WS rows: P.
Row 5: K10, K2tog, skp, K10—22 sts.
Row 7: K9, K2tog, skp, K9—20 sts.
Row 9: K8, K2tog, skp, K8—18 sts.
Row 11: With A, for sock, K7, K2tog, skp, K7—16 sts.
Row 13: K6, K2tog, skp, K6—14 sts.
Rows 15–16: K.
Rows 17–22: With C, St st.

CALF

Rows 23–28: St st, inc 1 st at beg of each row—20 sts.
Rows 29–32: St st.
Rows 33–38: St st, dec 1 st at beg of each row—14 sts.

LEG

Row 39: Kfb, k to last st, kfb—16 sts.
Rows 40–42: St st.
Rows 43–54: Rep Row 39–42 3 times—22 sts.
Row 55: BO next 10 sts, K to last 2 sts, K2tog—11 sts.
Rows 56–62: St st, dec 1 st at beg of each row—4 sts. BO.

LEFT LEG

Work same as Right Leg to Row 54 then work as follows:

Row 55: K.
Row 56: BO 10 sts p-wise, P to last 2 sts, P2tog—11 sts.
Rows 57–63: St st, dec 1 st at beg of each row—4 sts. BO.

Sew ends of rows tog for each leg working from top of leg to CO edge. Fold CO edge in half and whipstitch. Stuff legs firmly and sew to side of body as illustrated, adding more stuffing in the tops of legs as necessary.

ANTENNA (make 2)

With C, CO 5 sts

Rows 1–21: St st.
Row 22: With A, P.
Row 23: Kfb in each st across—10 sts.
Rows 24–28: St st.
Row 29: K2tog across—5 sts.

Cut yarn leaving a long tail, thread tail through rem sts, gather tightly and fasten off. Whip st ends of rows tog right side out, placing a small amount of stuffing in the A section. Sew antennae to top of head as illustrated.

ARMS (make 2)

With C, beg at shoulder, CO 6.

Rows 1–2, 15–22: St st.
Rows 3–12: St st, inc 1 st at beg of each row—16 sts.
Rows 13–14: St st, CO 2 at beg of each row—20 sts. Pm at each end of last row.
Row 23: [K1, K2tog, K1] across—15 sts.
Rows 24–50: St st.

HAND

Row 51: [K1, K2tog] across—10 sts.
Row 52: P.
Row 53: K2tog across—5 sts.

Cut yarn leaving a long tail, thread tail through rem sts, gather tightly and fasten off. Sew ends of rows tog for each arm working from hand to marker, stuff firmly. Sew top of arm to side of body as shown, adding more stuffing as necessary.

WINGS (make 2)

NOTE: Wings are worked sideways in garter st with two strands of A held tog throughout.

With A doubled and US 6 (4mm) needles, beg at center back, CO 28.

Rows 1, 7, 11: K.
Rows 2–6: K to last st, Kfb—38 sts.
Row 8: Kfb, K to last st, Kfb—40 sts.
Rows 9–10: Rep rows 7–8—42 sts.
Divide for wings

UPPER WING

Row 12: Kfb, K23, K2tog, turn—26 sts. Place rem 16 sts on holder.
Row 13: Skp, K to last st, Kfb.
Rows 14–18, 20–22, 24: K.
Row 19, 23: Skp, K to end—24 sts.
Rows 25–34: Kfb, K to last st, Kfb—4 sts. BO.

LOWER WING

Row 12: With right side facing and A held double, return rem 16 sts to needle and K across.
Rows 13–14: Kfb, K to last st, Kfb—20 sts.
Rows 15–16, 18–22: K.
Row 17: K to last st, Kfb—21 sts.
Row 23: K, dec 1 st at each end of row—19 sts.
Row 24: K.
Rows 25–34: Rep rows 23–24 5 times—7 sts.
Rows 35–36: Rep row 23—3 sts. BO.
Matching upper and lower wings, sew CO edges together. Sew seam to center back of body 3 rows above the stinger.

PLANT POT

With D doubled and US 2 (3mm) needles, beg at top, CO 48.

Rows 1–2: K.

Cut 1 strand and cont with only 1 strand of yarn.

Rows 3–10, 12–18, 20–25: St st.
Row 11: [K5, K2tog, K5] across—44 sts.
Row 19: [K4, K2tog, K5] across—40 sts.
Row 26: With 2 strands of yarn held tog, K.
Row 27: P

Cut one strand and cont with only 1 strand of yarn.

Rows 28–30: St st.

BASE

Row 31: [K2, K2tog] across—30 sts.
Row 32 and all WS rows: P.
Row 33: [K1, K2tog] across—20 sts.
Row 35: K2tog across—10 sts.

Cut yarn leaving a long tail, thread tail through rem sts, gather tightly and fasten off. Working from CO edge down, sew ends of rows tog. Stuff firmly.

SOIL

With F, CO 50.

Rows 1–3, 5–6: St st.
Row 4: K (outer edge of the soil)

CENTER TOP

Row 7: [K3, K2tog] across—40 sts.
Row 8 and all WS rows: P.
Row 9: [K2, K2tog] across—30 sts.
Row 11: [K1, K2tog] across—20 sts.
Row 13: K2tog across—10 sts.

Cut yarn leaving a long tail, thread tail through rem sts, gather tightly and fasten off. Sew ends of rows tog. Place the first 3 rows of St st down the inside of plant pot with row 4 just below the CO edge of pot. Sew in place.

FLOWERS (make 3)

With B, CO 11.

Row 1 (RS): K1, Kfb across—21 sts.
Rows 2–6, 8–10: St st.
Row 7 (Picot): K1, [yo, K2tog] across.
Rows 11–12: With H, St st.
Row 13: K1, K2tog across—11 sts.

Cut yarn leaving a long tail, thread tail through rem sts, gather tightly and fasten off. Sew ends of rows tog. Fold flowers at picot row, tightly gather CO st and sew to soil.

LEAVES (make 6)

With G, CO 11.

Rows 1–2: K8, turn and K to end.
Rows 3–4: K6, turn and K to end.
Row 5: K across all sts, BO.

Sew 2 leaves to the base of each flower.

FINISHING

Weave in all ends.

Colin the Caterpillar

Measurements
Length 15.5in/40.5cm, Height 8in/20cm

Materials

* Stylecraft Special DK 3.5oz/100g balls 100% Acrylic, one ball each:
  Bright Green 1259 (A), Matador 1010 (B), Green 1116 (C), White 1001
  (D), Turquoise 1068 (E), and Black 1002 (F)
* 5.25oz/150g Stuffing
* Stitch markers
* Knitting needles size US 2 (3mm)

Gauge
26 sts and 36 rows = 4in/10cm in St st.

BODY

With A, CO 12.

Row 1: K.
Row 2 and all WS rows: P.
Row 3: Kfb in each st across—24 sts.
Row 5: [Kfb, K1] across—36 sts.
Row 7: [K1, Kfb, K1] across—48 sts.
Row 9: [K1, Kfb, K2] across—60 sts.
Rows 11–30: St st.
Row 31: K3, K2tog 27 times, K3—33 sts.
Row 32: P4, pm in last st worked, P across to last 3 sts, pm in last st worked—gathering points on body marked.
Row 33: K3, Kfb 27 times, K3—60 sts.
Rows 35–56: St st.
Rows 57–134: Rep Rows 31–56 three times.
Row 135: K2, K2tog 28 times, K2—32 sts.
Row 136: P3, pm in last st worked, P across to last 2 sts, pm in last st worked.

NECK

Row 137: K15, yf, sl 1, yb, turn, leaving remaining sts unworked.
Row 138 and foll WS Rows: Sl 1, P across.
Row 139: K14, yf, sl 1, yb, turn.
Row 141: K13, yf, sl 1, yb, turn.
Rows 143–155: Cont as established working one less st at beg of RS rows.
Row 157: K5, yf, sl 1, yb, turn.
Row 159: K6, yf, sl 1, yb, turn.
Rows 161–175: Cont as established working one more st at beg of RS rows.
Row 177: K15, yf, sl 1, yb, turn.
Row 179: Knit across all sts—32 sts.
Row 180: P15, yb, sl 1, yf, turn.
Row 181 and foll RS Rows: Sl 1, K across.
Row 182: P14, yb, sl 1, yf, turn.
Rows 184–196: Cont as established working one less st at beg of WS rows.
Row 198: P5, yb, sl 1, yf, turn.
Row 200: P6, yb, sl 1, yf, turn.
Rows 202–216: Cont as established working one more st at beg of WS rows.
Row 218: P15, yb, sl 1, yf, turn.
Row 220: Purl across all sts—32 sts.
Rows 221–222, 224–228, 230–232: St st.
Row 223: [K1, K2tog, K1] across—24 sts.
Row 229: [K1, K2tog, K1] across —18 sts. BO.

Tightly gather CO sts and fasten off. Sew ends of rows tog creating a seam underneath body, stuffing body firmly before closing seam. With A doubled, gather body on marked rows.

HEAD

With A, CO 10.

Row 1: K.
Row 2 and all WS rows: P.
Row 3: Kfb across—20 sts.
Row 5: [Kfb, K1] across—30 sts.
Row 7: [K1, Kfb, K1] across—40 sts.
Row 9: [K1, Kfb, K2] across—50 sts.
Row 11: [K2, Kfb, K2] across—60 sts.
Rows 13–28: St st. Pm in center 2 sts of row 21.

HAT

Rows 29–42: With B, St st.

CROWN

Row 43: [K2, K2tog, K2] across—50 sts.
Row 45: [K1, K2tog, K2] across—40 sts.
Row 47: [K1, K2tog, K1] across—30 sts.
Row 49: [K1, K2tog] across—20 sts.
Row 51: K2tog across—10 sts.

Cut yarn leaving a long tail, thread tail through rem sts, gather tightly and fasten off. Tightly gather CO sts and fasten off. Sew ends of rows tog creating a seam at back of head. Stuff body firmly before closing seam. Sew head to top of neck at a slight angle.

HAT BRIM

With B, CO 65 for inner edge.

Rows 1, 3, 5, 6, 9, 11: P.
Row 2 (RS): K1, [Kfb, K1] across—97 sts.
Rows 4, 7, 8, 10: K.
Row 12: K1, [K2tog, K1] across—65 sts. BO.

Sew ends of rows tog. With RS out, whip st CO and bind off edges tog. Do not stuff. Sew brim to Row 29 of head, matching back seams.

FEET (make 10)

With C, CO 5.

Row 1: Kfb across—10 sts.
Rows 2–14: St st.
Row 15: K2tog across—5 sts.

Cut yarn leaving a long tail, thread tail through rem sts, gather tightly and fasten off. Tightly gather CO edge. With RS out, sew ends of rows tog along bottom of foot, stuffing firmly. Sew feet to either side of five body sections.

NOSE

With C, embroider 3 sts over marked sts on head.

MOUTH

With F, embroider a "V" of two long stitches worked out from st 6 rows below nose.

EYES (make 2)

With D, CO 12.

Rows 1–4: St st.
Row 5: With F, K2tog across—6 sts.

Cut yarn leaving a long tail, thread tail through rem sts, gather tightly and fasten off. Sew ends of rows tog and stuff firmly. Tightly gather CO sts and fasten off. With E, embroider a circle of 8 chain sts around F on each eye. With D, make a tiny straight stitch for the twinkle of each eye. Sew eyes 3 sts from center, 5 rows below hat.

ANTENNA (make 2)

With A, CO 5.
Rows 1–21: St st.
Row 22: With C, P.
Row 23: Kfb across—10 sts.
Rows 24–28: St st.
Row 29: K2tog across—5 sts.

Cut yarn leaving a long tail, thread tail through rem sts, gather tightly and fasten off. With RS out, whip st ends of rows tog, with a bit of stuffing in top section. Sew antennae to top of hat as pictured on page 13.

SCARF

With B, CO 4 and K 100 rows. BO and weave in ends. Tie scarf around neck as illustrated.

FINISHING

Weave in all ends.

Dippy the Duck

Measurements

Height 16in/41cm standing, 12in/30.5cm sitting

Materials

* Stylecraft Special DK 3.5oz/100g balls 100% Acrylic, one ball each:
  White 1001 (A), Sunshine 1114 (B), Matador 1010 (C), Jaffa 1256 (D),
  Bright Green 1259 (E), Turquoise 1068 (F), Royal 1117 (G), Grey 1099 (H),
  and Black 1002 (I)
* 7oz/200g Stuffing
* Stitch markers
* Knitting needles size US 2 (3mm)

Gauge

26 sts and 36 rows = 4in/10cm in St st.

BODY

With A, CO 12.

Rows 1–2, 8–10, 12–14, 16–20, 22–34, 36–42, 44–50, 52–56, 58–62: St st.
Row 3: Kfb across—24 sts.
Rows 4, 6: P.
Row 5: [Kfb, K1] across—36 sts.
Row 7: [K1, Kfb, K1] across—48 sts.
Row 11: [K1, Kfb, K2] across—60 sts.
Row 15: [K2, Kfb, K2] across—72 sts.
Row 21: [K2, Kfb, K3] across—84 sts.
Row 35: [K2, K2tog, K3] across, pm—72 sts.
Row 43: [K2, K2tog, K2] across—60 sts.
Row 51: [K1, K2tog, K2] across—48 sts.
Row 57: [K1, K2tog, K1] across—36 sts.

SHOULDERS

Row 63: K7, K2tog, skp, K14, K2tog, skp, K7—32 sts.
Rows 64, 66: P.
Row 65: K6, K2tog, skp, K12, K2tog, skp, K6—28 sts.
Row 67: K5, K2tog, skp, K10, K2tog, skp, K5—24 sts.
Rows 68–70: St st. BO.

Sew ends of rows tog, stuff firmly. Tightly gather CO edge and fasten off.

HEAD

With A, CO 24.

Row 1: K.
Rows 2, 4, 6: P.
Row 3: [Kfb, K1] across—36 sts.
Row 5: [K1, Kfb, K1] across—48 sts.

CHEEKS

Row 7: K9, Kfb 6 times, K18, Kfb 6 times, K9—60 sts.
Rows 8, 24: P
Row 9: K9, [Kfb, K1] 6 times, K18, [K1, Kfb] 6 times, K9—72 sts.
Rows 10–22: St st, pm in center 2 sts of rows 10 and 22.
Row 23: K9, [K2tog, K1] 6 times, K18, [K1, K2tog] 6 times, K9—60 sts.
Row 25: K9, K2tog 6 times, K18, K2tog 6 times, K9—48 sts.
Rows 26–36: St st.

TOP OF HEAD

Row 37: [K1, K2tog, K1] across—36 sts.
Rows 38–40: St st.
Row 41: [K1, K2tog] across—24 sts.
Row 42: P.
Row 43: K2tog across—12 sts.

Cut yarn leaving a long tail, thread tail through rem sts, gather tightly and fasten off. Sew ends of rows tog creating a seam underneath body, stuffing body firmly before closing seam. Tightly gather CO edge and fasten off.

BEAK (make 2)

With B, CO 22, pm in center st.

Rows 1–4: St st.
Rows 5–14: Cont in St st, dec 1 st at beg of each row—12 sts.
Rows 15–18: Cont in St st, dec 1 st at each end of row—4 sts.
BO. Sew pieces WS tog matching markers. Whip st across bound off edges. Sew ends of rows tog on both sides and stuff firmly. Sew CO edges to face centered at markers in rows 10 and 22 of head adding more stuffing as necessary.

EYES (make 2)

With A, CO 12.

Rows 1–4: St st.
Row 5: With I, K2tog across—6 sts.

Cut yarn leaving a long tail, thread tail through rem sts, gather tightly and fasten off. Sew ends of rows tog and stuff firmly. Tightly gather CO sts and fasten off. With F, embroider a circle of 8 chain sts around I on each eye. With A, make a tiny straight stitch for the twinkle in each eye. Sew eyes 2 sts from center, 7 rows above beak.

FEET (make 4)

With B, CO 8.

Rows 1–2: St st.
Rows 3–18: Cont in St st, inc 1 st at beg of each row – 24 sts.
Rows 19–30: St st. BO.

Sew 2 feet pieces WS tog, stuffing firmly. With B doubled make 2 long stitches through feet to indent toes as illustrated.

LEGS (make 2)

With B, CO 13. Work 26 rows St st, BO. Sew ends of rows tog and stuff firmly. Sew CO edge 0.5in/1cm in from center back edge of each foot. Sew legs to front of body.

WINGS (make 2)

With A, CO 20.

Rows 1–2, 4–6, 8–26, 28–30: St st.
Row 3: Kfb across—40 sts.
Row 7: [Kfb, K1] across—60 sts.
Row 27: [K2, K2tog, K2] across—50 sts.
Rows 31–66: Cont in St st, dec 1 st at beg of each row—14 sts.
Row 67: K2tog across—7 sts.

Cut yarn leaving a long tail, thread tail through rem sts, gather tightly and fasten off. Sew ends of rows tog, stuff lightly, whip st across CO edge. With the seam facing toward the back of duck, sew CO edges of each wing to either side of body at neck.

FEATHERS (make 1)

With A, CO 16.

Row 1: K.
Row 2: BO 13, K to end—3 sts.
Row 3: K3, CO 8—11 sts.
Row 4: BO 8, K to end—3 sts.
Row 5: K3, CO 12—15 sts. BO.
Sew straight row ends to top of head.

TAIL

OUTER PIECE (make 1)

With A, CO 6.

Rows 1–2, 9–12: St st.
Rows 3–8: Cont in St st, inc 1 st at each end of row—18 sts. Pm at each end of last row.
Rows 13–26: Cont in St st, dec 1 st at beg of row—4 sts. BO.

INNER PIECE (make 1)

With A, CO 18.

Rows 1–4: St st.
Rows 5–18: Cont in St st, dec 1 st at beg of row—4 sts. BO.

With WS tog matching markers of outer piece with CO edge of inner piece, Sew ends of rows tog and stuff firmly. Sew inc section of outer piece to base of body so the tail points upward.

LIFE PRESERVER RING (make 1)

Stripe Patt 14 rows C, D, B, E and F.

With C, CO 30.

Row 1: K.
Rows 2, 6, 10: P.
Row 3: K26, yf, sl 1, yb, turn.
Row 4: Sl 1, P22, yb, sl 1, yf, turn.
Rows 5, 9: Sl 1, K29.
Row 7: K22, yf, sl 1, yb, turn.
Row 8: Sl 1, P14, yb, sl 1, yf, turn.
Row 11: K18, yf, sl 1, yb, turn.
Row 12: Sl 1, P6, yb, sl 1, yf, turn.
Row 13: Sl 1, K across all sts.
Row 14: P 30, change to next color.

Rep Rows 1–14 14 times.
Ending with F, work 2 rows St st.
BO. Sew CO and BO edges tog. Sew ends of rows tog, stuffing firmly. Place legs and body through middle of life preserver ring and sew inner edge to row 35 of body.

PATCH (make 1)

With G, CO 8, work 9 rows Rev St st, BO. Sew patch just off center front of life preserver ring. With H, embroider a few straight stitches unevenly around patch and onto life preserver ring.

FINISHING

Weave in all ends.

Dottie the Ladybug

Measurements

Length 8in/20cm, Height 3.5in/9cm

Materials

* Stylecraft Special DK 3.5oz/100g balls 100% Acrylic, one ball each:
  Matador 1010 (A), Black 1002 (B), and White 1001 (C)
* 3.5oz/100g Stuffing
* Stitch markers
* Knitting needles size US 2 (3mm)

Gauge

26 sts and 36 rows = 4in/10cm St st.

BODY

With A, cast on 12 sts.

Rows 1–2, 4, 6–8, 10–12, 14–18, 20–24, 26–42, 44–52, 54: St st.
Row 3: Kfb in each st across—24 sts.
Row 5: [Kfb, K1] across—36 sts.
Row 9: [K1, Kfb, K1] across—48 sts.
Row 13: [K1, Kfb, K2] across—60 sts.
Row 19: [K2, Kfb, K2] across—72 sts.
Row 25: [K2, Kfb, K3] across —84 sts.
Row 43: [K2, K2tog, K3] across—72 sts.
Row 53: [K2, K2tog, K2] across—60 sts.
Rows 55–62: Change to B for head, St st, pm at center of row 55.
Row 63 [K1, K2tog, K2] across—48 sts.
Rows 64–70, 72–76, 78–80: St st.
Row 71: [K1, K2tog, K1] across—36 sts.
Row 77: [K1, K2tog] across—24 sts.
Row 81: K2tog across—12 sts.

Cut yarn leaving a long tail, thread tail through rem sts, gather tightly and fasten off. Tightly gather cast on sts and sew ends of rows tog creating a seam underneath body, stuffing body firmly before closing seam. Flatten to shape body. With a length of B doubled embroider a straight line of chain sts from marker to gathered sts at the back of body.

MOUTH

With A, embroider a "V" of two long stitches worked out from st 2 rows above gathered cast on sts.

EYES (make 2)

With C, CO 16 sts, K 1 row.

Next row: P2tog across—8 sts.

Cut yarn leaving a long tail, thread tail through rem sts, gather tightly and fasten off. Sew ends of rows tog. With B, embroider a circle of 8 chain sts around C on each eye, leaving a small section of C showing as illustrated. Sew eyes 5 rows below 1st B row, 2 sts either side of marker.

SPOTS (make 7)

With B, CO 24 sts. Work 2 rows in St st.

Next row: K2tog across—12 sts.

Cut yarn leaving a long tail, thread tail through rem sts, gather tightly and fasten off. Sew ends of rows tog to form a circle. Backstitch around outer cast on edge to sew 3 spots either side of central B line on back of body as illustrated with the final spot on center line of back.

FINISHING

Weave in all ends.

Freddie the Fire Engine

Measurements
Length 13in/33cm, Height 9in/23cm, Width 6in/15cm

Materials
* Stylecraft Special DK 3.5oz/100g balls 100% Acrylic one ball each:
  Matador 1010 (A), Black 1002 (B), White 1001 (C), Sunshine 1114 (D),
  Silver 1203 (E), Aster 1003 (F), Jaffa 1256 (G), and Claret 1123 (H)
* 8.8oz/250g Stuffing
* Three 5mm plastic drinking straws
* Knitting needles size US 2 (3mm)

Gauge
26 sts and 36 rows = 4in/10cm in St st.

BODY

RIGHT SIDE

With A CO 75.

Rows 1–6: St st.

REFLECTIVE SQUARES

Rows 7–18: Work in fair isle method following color chart A.
Rows 19–28: Cont with A only in St st.
Row 29: BO 17 sts for hood shaping, K across—58 sts.
Row 30: P.

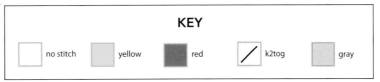

KEY

| | no stitch | | yellow | | red | / | k2tog | | gray |

CHART A

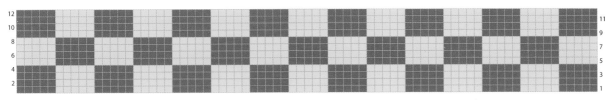

WINDOW

Rows 31–56: Work St st in intarsia method following color chart B with the following shaping at the beg of indicated rows:
Row 35: K2tog—57 sts.
Row 39: K2tog—56 sts.
Row 43: K2tog—55 sts.
Row 46: BO 32—23 sts.
Row 47: K2tog—22 sts.
Row 51: K2tog—21 sts.
Row 55: K2tog—20 sts.
Rows 57–58: Cont with A only, St st.
Row 59: K2tog, K across—19 sts.
Rows 60–62: St st, BO.

CHART B

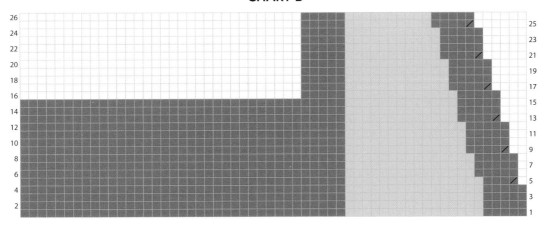

LEFT SIDE

Work as for right side, working K as P and P as K throughout.

BODY PANEL

With A CO 38 sts.

Rows 1–2: St st.

WINDSHIELD Work in intarsia method.

Row 3: K3 A, 32 C, 3 A.
Row 4: P3 A, 32 C, 3 A.
Rows 5–28: Rep Row 3-4 12 times.
Rows 29–34: Cont with A only, St st.
Rows 35–36: P for fold at roof edge.
Rows 37–58: St st.
Rows 59–60: P for fold at back of cab.
Rows 61–76: St st.
Rows 77–78: P for fold at trailer roof.
Rows 79–118: St st.
Rows 119–120: P for fold at tailgate.
Rows 121–166: St st.
Rows 167–168: P for fold at back bumper.
Rows 169–258: With B, St st.
Rows 259–260: With A, K for fold at front bumper.
Rows 261–288: St st.
Rows 289–290: P for fold at hood.
Rows 291–310: St st, BO.

Weave in ends for colorwork sections. Sew CO and BO edges tog to form a tube. Sew body sides to ends of rows aligning P row fold lines to corner points on side piece as illustrated, stuffing firmly before closing seam. With C, chain stitch the word 'FIRE' on both sides of truck starting 7 st from window edge.

WHEELS (make 4)

With B CO 5.

Row 1: K.
Row 2 and all WS rows: (unless otherwise indicated) P.
Row 3: Kfb across—10 sts.
Row 5: [Kfb, K1] across—15 sts.
Row 7: [K1, Kfb, K1] across—20 sts.
Row 9: [K1, Kfb, K2] across—25 sts.

WHEEL TREAD

Rows 11–13: K.
Rows 14–20: St st.
Row 21: P.

OUTER SIDE

Row 22: CO 25, P across—50 sts.
Rows 23–24: St st.
Row 25: [K1, K2tog, K2] across—40 sts.
Row 27: [K1, K2tog, K1] across—30 sts.
Row 28: With E, P.
Row 29: [K1, K2tog] across—20 sts.
Row 31: K2tog across—10 sts.

Cut yarn leaving a long tail, thread tail through rem sts, gather tightly and fasten off. Seam outer side section to form a circle. Tightly gather CO edge of inner wheel and fasten off. Sew in place 10 sts in from front or back edge of truck, backstitch CO edge of each outer wheel to truck sides. Stuff the inner wheel firmly and sew tread and inner wheel edges to truck base.

RADIATOR GRILL

With E, CO 16.

Row 1: K.
Row 2: P2, K12, P2.
Rows 3–20: Rep row 1-2.
Rows 21–23: St st, BO.

Sew to center front below hood fold.

HEADLIGHTS (make 2)

With E, CO 15.

Rows 1–2: With C, St st.

Cut yarn leaving a long tail, thread tail through rem sts, gather tightly and fasten off.

INDICATOR LIGHTS (make 4)

With E, CO 11, change to G and K 1 row.

Cut yarn leaving a long tail, thread tail through rem sts, gather tightly and fasten off.

BRAKE LIGHTS (make 2)

With E, CO 12, change to H and K 1 row.

Next row: P2tog across—6 sts.

Cut yarn leaving a long tail, thread tail through rem sts, gather tightly and fasten off.

BLUE LIGHTS (make 2)

With E, CO 16.

Rows 1–6: With F, St st.
Row 7: K2tog across—8 sts.

Cut yarn leaving a long tail, thread tail through rem sts, gather tightly and fasten off.
Sew side edges of every light, sew headlights and two indicator lights to truck front, and brake lights and the other two indicator lights to back of truck. Stuff blue lights firmly and sew to roof, backstitching in place.

LADDER

Sides (make 2)

With E, CO 5, work 70 rows in St st.

Cut yarn leaving a long tail, thread tail through rem sts, gather tightly and fasten off.

RUNGS (make 6)

With E, CO 5, work 14 rows in St st.

Cut yarn leaving a long tail, thread tail through rem sts, gather tightly and fasten off.
Cut 2 pieces of drinking straw 8.25in/21cm and five 1.5in/4cm for the rungs. Whip st strips around straw pieces. Sew rungs evenly spaced along two side pieces. Sew ladder between the blue lights and at back edge of trailer roof.

FINISHING

Weave in all ends.

Henry the Hedgehog

Measurements

Grass 8in/20cm square; Hedgehog Length 5.5in/14.5cm, Height 3.5in/9cm
Ladybug Length 1.5in/3cm; Toadstool Height 3.5in/9cm

Materials

* Stylecraft Special DK 3.5oz/100g balls 100% Acrylic, one ball each:
  Meadow 1065 (A), Khaki 1027 (B), Stone 1710 (C), Walnut 1054 (D),
  Matador 1010 (E), White 1001 (F), Black 1002 (G), and Sunshine 1114 (H)
* 2.5oz [70g] Stuffing
* 2.5in/6cm diameter piece of thick white cardboard
* Clear adhesive
* Knitting needles size US 2 (3mm), US 6 (4mm) and US 8 (5mm)

Gauge

26 sts and 36 rows = 4in/10cm in St st with US 2 (3mm) needles.

NOTE: Use US 2 (3mm) needles, unless otherwise stated.

HEDGEHOG

With D and C held together and US 6 (4mm) needles, CO 8.

Row 1 and all RS rows of body: P.
Row 2: Kfb across—16 sts.
Row 4: [Kfb, K1] across—24 sts.
Row 6: [K1, Kfb, K1] across—32 sts.
Row 8: [K1, Kfb, K2] across—40 sts.
Rows 10–27: Rev St st.

BODY

Row 28: [K1, K2tog, K1] across—30 sts.
Rows 29–31: Rev St st.
Row 32: [K1, K2tog, K2] across—24 sts.

HEAD

Change to US 2 (3mm) needles, cut D and cont with only C.

Rows 33–36: St st.

SNOUT

Row 37: K10, K2tog, skp, K10—22 sts.
Row 38 and all WS rows of snout: P.
Row 39: K9, K2tog, skp, K9—20 sts.
Row 41: K8, K2tog, skp, K8—18 sts.
Row 43: K7, K2tog, skp, K7—16 sts.
Row 45: K6, K2tog, skp, K6—14 sts.
Row 47: K5, K2tog, skp, K5—12 sts.
Row 49: K4, K2tog, skp, K4—10 sts.

NOSE

Rows 50–52: With D, St st.
Row 53: K2tog across—5 sts.

Cut yarn leaving a long tail, thread tail through rem sts, gather tightly and fasten off. Sew ends of rows tog creating a seam underneath body, stuffing body firmly before closing seam.

LEGS (make 4)

With C, CO 10, work 4 rows St st.

Change to D and work 2 rows St st.

Next row: K2tog across—5 sts.

Cut yarn leaving a long tail, thread tail through rem sts, gather tightly and fasten off. Sew ends of rows tog. Stuff firmly and sew CO edge to underbody.

EYES

With a length of G, embroider a circle of 3 chain stitches for each eye.

GRASS

With A and B held together and US 8 (5mm) needles, CO 37.

Rows 1–64: K1, [P1, K1] across. BO in patt, weave in ends.

FLOWERS (make 3)

With F, CO 12, K 1 row. Cut yarn leaving a long tail, thread tail through sts, gather tightly and fasten off. Sew ends of rows tog. Sew to grass as pictured on page 29. With H, work a large French knot in the center of each flower.

LEAVES (make 3)

With A, CO 10, BO. Sew leaves to flowers.

FINISHING

Weave in all ends.

TOADSTOOL

GILLS

With F, CO 61.

Rows 1, 3: K1, [P3, K1] across.
Row 2: P1, [K3, P1] across.
Row 4: P1, [K1, K2tog, P1] across—46 sts.
Row 5: K1, [P2, K1] across.
Row 6: P1, [K2tog, P1] across—31 sts.
Row 7: K1, [P1, K1] across.
Row 8: P1, [P2tog] across—16 sts.
Row 9: K.
Row 10: P2tog across—8 sts.

Cut yarn leaving a long tail, thread tail through rem sts, gather tightly and fasten off.

CAP

With E and RS facing, pick up and K 61 sts from CO edge of gills.

Row 1 and all WS rows: P.
Row 2: K1, [K2, Kfb, K3] across—71 sts.
Row 4: K.
Row 6: K1, [K2, K2tog, K3] across—61 sts.
Row 8: K1, [K2, K2tog, K2] across—51 sts.
Row 10: K1, [K1, K2tog, K2] across—41 sts.
Row 12: K1, [K1, K2tog, K1] across—31 sts.
Row 14: K1, [K2tog, K1] across—21 sts.
Row 16: K1, K2tog across—11 sts.

Cut yarn leaving a long tail, thread tail through rem sts, gather tightly and fasten off. Sew ends of rows tog, leaving gills open. Cut a 2.5in/6cm diameter circle of thick white cardboard, glue inside gills. Stuff firmly and sew closed. With F, embroider random circles on cap.

STEM

With F, CO 14.

Rows 1–14: St st.
Rows 15–16: With A, St st.
Row 17: [Kfb, K1] across—21 sts.
Rows 18, 20–22, 24, 26: P.
Row 19: [K1, Kfb, K1] across—28 sts.
Row 23: [K1, K2tog, K1] across—21 sts.
Row 25: [K1, K2tog] across—14 sts.
Row 27: K2tog across—7 sts.

Cut yarn leaving a long tail, thread tail through rem sts, gather tightly and fasten off. Sew ends of rows tog. Stuff firmly and sew CO edge to center gills. With A, embroider lines to imitate grass as pictured on page 32. Sew to grass at row 21.

LADYBUG

With E, CO 10.

Rows 1–2, 4–10: St st.
Row 3: Kfb across—20 sts.
Rows 11–14: With G, St st.
Row 15: [K1, K2tog, K1] across—15 sts.
Row 16: P.
Row 17: [K1, K2tog] across—10 sts.
Row 18: P2tog across—5 sts.

Cut yarn leaving a long tail, thread tail through rem sts, gather tightly and fasten off. Sew ends of rows tog. Stuff firmly. Tightly gather CO edge and fasten off. With G, embroider a line from row 11 at center of body as shown. Sew ladybug onto grass as pictured on p. 29.

SPOTS

With G, embroider 2 circles of 5 chain sts on either side center back line.

FACE

With E, stitch a tiny "V" for the mouth and a few horizontal lines for the nose. With F, embroider one chain st for each eye.

Jacob the Bear

Measurements

Height 9in/23cm

Materials

* Stylecraft Special DK 3.5oz/100g balls 100% Acrylic, one ball each: Camel 1420 (A), Walnut 1054 (B), Meadow 1065 (C), Khaki 1027 (D), and Black 1002 (E)
* 6.35oz/180g Stuffing
* Stitch markers
* Knitting needles size US 2 (3mm) and US 8 (5mm)

Gauge

26 sts and 36 rows = 4in/10cm in St st with US 2 (3mm) needles.

NOTE: Use US 2 (3mm) needles throughout, unless otherwise stated.

BODY

With A, CO 12.

Rows 1, 9: K.
Row 2 and all WS rows: P.
Row 3: Kfb in each st across—24 sts.
Row 5: [Kfb, K1] across—36 sts.
Row 7: [K1, Kfb, K1] across—48 sts.
Row 11: [K1, Kfb, K2] across—60 sts.

TUMMY

Row 13: K28, Kfb, pm, K2, pm, Kfb, K28—62 sts.
Rows 15–23: St st, inc before1st marker and after 2nd on RS rows—72 sts.
Rows 24–38: Remove markers, St st.
Row 39: K34, K2tog, pm, skp, K34—70 sts.
Rows 41–49: St st, dec before and after marker—60 sts.
Row 51: K.

SIDES OF BODY

Row 53: [K2, K2tog, K2] across—50 sts.
Row 55: K.
Row 57: [K2, K2tog, K1] across—40 sts.

SHOULDERS

Row 59: K6, K2tog 4 times, K12, K2tog 4 times, K6—32 sts.
Rows 60–63: St st, BO.

Sew ends of rows tog, tightly gather CO sts and fasten off. Stuff body firmly.

HEAD

With A, starting at snout, CO 12.

Row 1: K.
Row 3: Kfb in each st across—24 sts.
Row 5: K7, Kfb, pm, K8, pm Kfb, K7—26 sts.
Rows 7–13: St st, inc before 1st marker and after 2nd on RS rows—34 sts.

FACE

Row 15: Remove markers, Kfb, [K1, Kfb] 6 times, K8, Kfb, [K1, Kfb] 6 times—48 sts.
Row 17: K16, Kfb, pm, K2, pm, Kfb, K8, Kfb, pm, K2, pm, Kfb, K16—52 sts. Pm through center sts for eye position.
Rows 19–27: K to m, Kfb, K2, Kfb, K to m, Kfb, K2, Kfb, K to end—72 sts.
Row 29: K2, [Kfb, K3] 5 times, Kfb, K2, Kfb, K20, Kfb, K2, Kfb, [K3, Kfb] 5 times, K2—86 sts. Pm for ear position 8 sts from center on each side.
Rows 30–44: St st.

BACK OF HEAD

Row 45: K1, [K2, K2tog, K2] to last st, K1—72 sts.
Row 47: K1, [K1, K2tog, K2] to last st, K1—58 sts.
Row 49: K1, [K1, K2tog, K1] to last st, K1—44 sts.
Row 51: K1, [K2tog, K1] to last st, K1—30 sts.
Row 53: K2tog across—5 sts.

Cut yarn leaving a long tail, thread tail through rem sts, gather tightly and fasten off. Tightly gather CO edge and fasten off. Sew ends of rows tog, creating a seam underneath head, stuffing body firmly before closing seam. Sew head to top of neck opening as illustrated. With E, embroider a circle of 5 chain sts for each eye 3 sts to either side of marker.

NOSE

With B, CO 10.

Rows 1–2: St st.
Rows 3–6: St st, dec 1 st at each end of row—2 sts.
Row 7: K2tog, cut yarn, leaving a long tail, and fasten off. Sew nose to snout as illustrated. With E, embroider mouth.

EARS

OUTER EAR (make 2 with A for outer and 2 with B for inner)

With A, CO 14.

Rows 1–6: St st.
Rows 7–10: St st, dec 1 st at each end of row—6 sts. BO.

Sew edges of outer and inner ear in pairs. Sew CO edge of ears in a slightly curved shape to the outside of the markers in row 29 of head.

ARMS

RIGHT ARM

With A, CO 14.

Rows 1–2, 4–8, 11–22: St st.
Row 3: [Kfb, K1] across—21 sts.
Rows 9–10: St st, CO 2 at beg of row—25 sts. Pm at each end of last row.
Row 23: [K5, K2tog] 3 times, K4—22 sts.
Row 33: K6, [K2tog, K6] 2 times—20 sts.

PAW

1ST SIDE

Row 37: K9, Kfb, turn.
Rows 38–40: Working on 11 sts only, St st.
Rows 41–46: St St, dec 1 st at beg of row—5 sts. BO.

2ND SIDE

With RS facing, join F to row 37 and work across rem 10 sts, Kfb, K9—11 sts. Rep Rows 38–46 of 1st side.

LEFT ARM Rep rows 1–36 of right arm.

PAWS

Rep as rows 37–46 of right arm joining B for 1st side and A for 2nd side. Sew around paw. Sew ends of rows tog to markers leaving top edge open. Stuff firmly and sew open edge to top of body.

LEGS (make 2)

With A, CO 46.

Rows 1–10: St st.
Row 11: K13, K2tog 10 times, K13—36 sts.
Row 12: P.
Row 13: K12, K2tog 6 times, K12—30 sts.
Row 14: P, pm at center front.
Row 15: K10, BO 10 sts for top of foot, K across—20 sts.
Rows 16–22: St st, working across all sts—20 sts.
Row 23: [K2, Kfb, K2] across—24 sts.
Rows 24–28, 30–34, 36–42: St st.
Row 29: [K2, Kfb, K3] across—28 sts.
Row 35: [K3, Kfb, K3] across—32 sts.
Row 43: K1, [skp, K11, K2tog] 2 times, K1—28 sts.
Rows 44, 46, 48: P.
Row 45: K1, [skp, K9, K2tog] 2 times, K1—24 sts.
Row 47: K1, [skp, K7, K2tog] 2 times, K1—20 sts.
Row 49: K1, [skp, K5, K2tog] 2 times, K1—16 sts.
Row 50: P, BO.

Sew ends of rows tog from foot to hip leaving a 1in/2.5cm gap at top. Fold BO sts in row 15 half using marker as a guide and sew BO edges tog at top of foot.

SOLES (make 2)

With B, CO 6.

Rows 1–2, 5–16: St st.
Rows 3–4: St st, inc 1 st at each end of row—10 sts.
Rows 17–18: St st, dec 1 st at each end of row—6 sts. BO.

Sew sole to CO edge of leg, stuff leg firmly. Sew legs to lower edge of body.

SWEATER

Stripe patt: 4 rows C, St st; 2 rows D, K.

BODY (make 2)

With D, CO 55.

Rows 1–4: 1/1 Rib K1, [P1, K1] across.
Row 5: Begin Stripe patt; dec 1 st at each end of row—53 sts.
Rows 6–32: Maintaining Stripe patt, dec 1 st at each end of every 3rd row 9 times—35 sts.
Rows 33–42: Work even in Stripe patt.

SHOULDERS

Rows 43–44: Maintaining Stripe patt, BO 7 sts at beg of each row—21 sts.

NECKBAND

Rows 45–48: With D, 1/1 Rib, BO loosely in rib using US 8 (5mm) needle.

SLEEVES (make 2)

With D, CO 27.

Rows 1–2: 1/1 Rib.
Row 3: Begin Stripe patt, inc 1 st at each end of row—29 sts.
Rows 4–8: Work even in Stripe patt.
Row 9: Maintaining Stripe patt, inc 1 st at each end of row—31 sts.
Rows 10–18: Work even in Stripe patt.

BO loosely with C. Sew in sleeves. Sew side and sleeve seams. Place sweater on teddy.

FINISHING

Weave in all ends.

Marvin the Mouse

Measurements

Height 8in/20cm

Materials

* Stylecraft Special DK 3.5oz [100g] balls 100% Acrylic, one ball each: Royal 1117 (A), Grey 1099 (B), Silver 1203 (C), Black 1002 (D), Matador 1010 (E), White 1001 (F), and Apricot 1026 (G)
* 1.4oz [40g] Stuffing
* Stitch holder
* Knitting needles size US 2 (3mm)

Gauge

26 sts and 36 rows = 4in/10cm in St st.

LEGS AND BODY

LEGS (make 2)

With B, CO 11.

Rows 1–2: St st.
Row 3: K3, [Kfb, K3] 2 times—13 sts.
Row 4: P.
Rows 5–6: With A, K.
Row 7: K3, [Kfb, K1] 3 times, Kfb, K3—17 sts.
Rows 8–10: St st.
Row 11: K3, [Kfb, K2] 3 times, Kfb, K4—21 sts.
Row 12: P. Slip 21 sts onto st holder.

JOINING LEGS

Row 13: K across 21 sts from each st holder—42 sts. Pm at each end of row.
Row 14: P.

TUMMY

Row 15: K4, [Kfb, K3] 4 times, K5, [Kfb, K3] 4 times, K1—50 sts.
Rows 16–30: St st.
Rows 31–32: K for waistband.

UPPER BODY

Stripe Patt: 2 rows E, 2 rows F

Working in stripe patt:

Rows 33–46, 48–50, 52, 54: St st.
Row 47: K9, K2tog 4 times, K16, K2tog 4 times, K9—42 sts.
Row 51: [K1, K2tog] across—28 sts.
Row 53: K2tog across—14 sts.
Row 54: P across, BO.

Sew ends of rows tog to markers. Seam back of body stuffing legs and body firmly before closing.

FEET (make 2)

With B, CO 6
Rows 1–2, 4–12: St st.
Row 3: Kfb in each st across—12 sts.
Rows 13–16: With C, St st.
Row 17: K2tog across—6 sts.

Cut yarn leaving a long tail, thread tail through rem sts, gather tightly and fasten off. Sew ends of rows tog creating seam underneath foot. Stuff lightly, tightly gather CO edge and fasten off. Sew each foot pointing outward slightly with back edge 2 rows in from CO edge, making sure the mouse will be able to stand.

TAIL

With B, CO 6.
Rows 1–10, 12–20, 22–32: St st.
Row 11: K2, K2tog, K2—5 sts.
Row 21: K2, K2tog, K1—4 sts.
Row 33: With C, K1, K2tog, K1—3 sts.
Rows 34–42: St st.
Row 43: K2tog, K1—2 sts.
Rows 44–48: St st.

Cut yarn leaving a long tail, thread tail through rem sts, gather tightly and fasten off. Sew ends of row tog with RS out. Sew CO edge to back, lower edge of body.

ARMS (make 2)

With E, CO 12, pm at center.

Rows 1–20: St st in Stripe patt.
Row 21: With E, [K1, K2tog] across—8 sts.
Row 22: K for cuff.
Rows 23–28: With B, St st for hand.
Row 29: K2tog across—4 sts.

Cut yarn leaving a long tail, thread tail through rem sts, gather tightly and fasten off. Seam hand and arm to form a tube, stuffing hand firmly and arm lightly as you seam. Fold CO edge in half and sew to upper body on the second E stripe from top of shoulders, making sure the arms are pointing downward.

HEAD

With B, CO 8.

Row 1: K.
Row 2 and all WS rows: P.
Row 3: Kfb in each st across—16 sts.
Row 5: [Kfb, K1] across—24 sts.
Row 7: [K1, Kfb, K1] across—32 sts.
Row 9: [K1, Kfb, K2] across—40 sts.
Rows 10–16: St st.

Face color detail in intarsia method following color chart for rows 17–35 or work as follows:

Row 17: K2 C, 36 B, 2 C.
Row 18: P3 C, 34 B, 3 C.
Row 19: K4 C, 32 B, 4 C.
Row 20: P6 C, 28 B, 6 C.
Row 21: K8 C, 24 B, 8 C.
Row 22: P11 C, 18 B, 11 C.

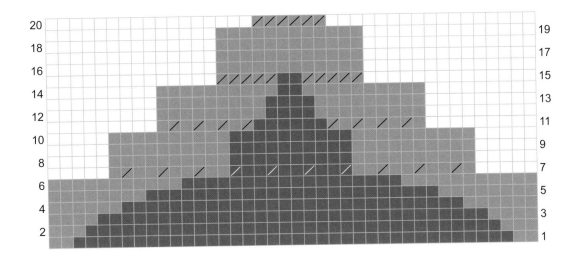

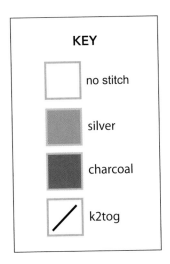

KEY

☐ no stitch

◻ silver

◼ charcoal

╱ k2tog

SNOUT

Row 23: With C, K1, [K2tog, K2] 3 times. With B, [K2tog, K2] 3 times, K2tog. With C [K2, K2tog] 3 times, K1—30 sts.
Row 24: P10 C, 10 B, 10 C.
Row 25: K10 C, 10 B, 10 C.
Row 26: P10 C, 10 B, 10 C.
Row 27: With C, [K1, K2tog] 4 times. With B, K6. With C, [K2tog, K1] 4 times—22 sts.
Row 28: P9 C, 4 B, 9 C.
Row 29: K9 C, 4 B, 9 C.
Row 30: P10 C, 2 B, 10 C.
Row 31: With C, K2tog 5 times. With B, K2. With C, K2tog 5 times—12 sts.
Rows 32–34: Cont with C only, St st.
Row 35: K2tog across—6 sts.

Cut yarn leaving a long tail, thread tail through rem sts, gather tightly and fasten off. Sew ends of rows tog creating a seam underneath head. Stuff head firmly before closing seam. Sew head to top of body.

EARS (make 2)

With C, CO 16.

Rows 1–2: St st.

Row 3: K2tog across—8 sts.

Cut yarn leaving a long tail, thread tail through rem sts, gather tightly and fasten off. Sew ends of rows tog. WS facing forward, sew ears to either side of head.

FACE

With B, stitch indents for eye. With D, stitch a French knot in each eye. With G, make a few straight stitches over center 2 sts for the nose.

OVERALL STRAPS (make 2)

With A, CO 40, K 1 row, BO.
Sew ends of straps 8 sts apart, to edge of waistband on overalls at front as illustrated. Cross straps on back of body and sew 10 sts apart on back edge of overalls.

FINISHING

Weave in all ends.

Mrs. Hopper the Rabbit

Measurements

Height 11in/28cm

Materials

* Stylecraft Special DK 3.5oz/100g balls 100% Acrylic, one ball each: White 1001 (A), Camel 1420 (B), Fondant 1241 (C), Dark Brown 1004 (D), Spice 1711 (E), Walnut 1054 (F), and Meadow 1065 (G)
* 6.35oz/180g Stuffing
* Stitch markers
* Knitting needles size US 2 (3mm)

Gauge

26 sts and 36 rows = 4in/10cm in St st.

BODY

BACK

With A, CO 14.

Row 1: K.
Row 2 and all WS rows: P.
Row 3: Kfb in each st across—28 sts.
Row 5: [Kfb, K1] across—42 sts.
Row 7: [K1, Kfb, K1] across—56 sts.
Rows 8–38: St st.

SHAPE BODY

Row 39: [K3, K2tog, K3] across—49 sts.
Rows 40–46, 48–54, 56–62, 64–68: St st.
Row 47: [K3, K2tog, K2] across—42 sts.
Row 55: [K2, K2tog, K2] across—35 sts.
Row 63: [K2, K2tog, K1] across—28 sts.
Row 69: [K1, K2tog, K1] across—21 sts.
Rows 70–72: St st, BO neck edge.

FRONT

With B, CO 12.

Row 1: K.
Row 2 and all WS rows: P.
Row 3: Kfb in each st across—24 sts.
Row 5: K1, [Kfb, K2] to last 2 sts, Kfb, K1—32 sts.
Row 7: K1, [Kfb, K3] to last 3 sts, Kfb, K2—40 sts.
Rows 8–36, 38–44, 46–52, 54–60, 62–66: St st.
Row 37: [K3, K2tog, K3] across—35 sts.
Row 45: [K3, K2tog, K2] across—30 sts.
Row 53: [K2, K2tog, K2] across—25 sts.
Row 61: [K2, K2tog, K1] across—20 sts.
Row 67: [K1, K2tog, K1] across—15 sts.
Rows 68–70: St st. BO neck edge.

Sew ends of rows tog on body, stuff body, tightly gather CO sts and fasten off.

FEET

UPPERS (make 2)

With A, CO 48.

Rows 1–4: St st.

SHAPE FOOT

Rows 5–8: St st, dec 1 st at each end of each row—40 sts.
Rows 9–12: St st, BO 4 sts at beg of each row—16 sts.
Row 13: [K1, K2tog, K1] across—12 sts.
Row 14: P, BO.

Sew ends of rows tog for front edge, matching BO shaping.

SOLES (make 2)

With B, CO 4.

Row 1: P.
Rows 2–5: St st, inc 1 st at each end of each row—12 sts.
Rows 6–25: St st.
Rows 26–28: St st, dec 1 st at each end of each row—6 sts.
Row 29: P, BO.

Sew edges of each sole to CO edge of each foot. Stuff firmly. Sew across BO sts and sew each foot to lower edge of body.

HEAD

With A, CO 36 at neck edge.

Rows 1–2, 4–6: St st.
Row 3: [K1, Kfb, K1] across—48 sts.
Rows 7–12: St st, inc 1 st at each end of each row—60 sts.
Rows 13–16: St st, pm in each end of last row.

SIDES OF HEAD

Rows 17–30: St st, dec 1 st at each end of each row—32 sts.
Row 31: [K1, K2tog, K1] across—24 sts.
Row 32: P.
Rows 33–36: St st, BO 3 sts at beg of each row—12 sts.

HEAD GUSSET

Rows 37–48: With B, St st.
Row 49: St st, dec 1 st at each end of row.
Rows 50–52: St st.
Rows 53–68: Rep last 4 rows 4 times—2 sts. BO.

Sew ends of rows 1–16 tog. Sew gusset sides to the shaped row ends of head and stuff firmly. With A make a stitch through the face and stuffing where the eyes will be sewn, pull up tightly to create indentations and fasten off securely. Sew CO edge of head to BO edges of body.

EARS (make 2 with A for outer and 2 with B for inner)

With A, CO 12 for base edge.

Rows 1–6, 8–22: St st.
Row 7: [Kfb, K1] across—18 sts.
Row 23: St st, dec 1 st at each end of row—16 sts.
Rows 24–28: St st.
Rows 29–58: Rep last 6 rows 5 times.
Row 59: Rep row 23—4 sts.
Rows 60–62: St st, BO.

Sew ends of rows tog of one outer ear and one inner ear matching CO and BO edges. Fold CO edge in half and sew ends of rows 1–6 tog. Sew ears to sides of head gusset.

NOSE

With D, CO 7 for top edge.

Rows 1–2: St st.
Rows 3–4: St st, dec 1 st at each end of row—3 sts.
Row 5: K3tog, fasten off.

Sew nose to gusset with bottom of nose at the last row of the gusset. With D, embroider mouth.

EYES (make 2)

With F, CO 12.

Rows 1–5: St st.
Row 6: P2tog across—6 sts.

Cut yarn leaving a long tail, thread tail through rem sts, gather tightly and fasten off. Tightly gather CO sts and fasten off. Sew ends of rows tog, stuffing firmly before closing. Sew eyes in indentations on head. With A, make a tiny stitch on each eye for the twinkle.

TAIL

With A, CO 10.

Rows 1–2, 4–12: St st.
Row 3 (WS): Kfb in each st across—20 sts.
Row 13: K2tog across—10 sts.

Cut yarn leaving a long tail, thread tail through rem sts, gather tightly and fasten off. Tightly gather CO sts and fasten off. Sew ends of rows tog, stuffing firmly before closing. Note: Purl side is RS. Sew tail to back of body.

CARDIGAN

With C, CO 92.

Rows 1–5: K.
Row 6 (WS): K3, P to last 3 sts, K3.
Rows 7–12: Rep row 5–6.
Row 13: K3, [K6, K2tog] to last 9 sts, K9—82 sts.
Row 14: K3, P to last 3 sts, K3.
Row 15: K.
Rows 16–20, 22–26, 28–32, 34–36, 38: Rep rows 14–15.
Row 21: K3, [K5, K2tog] to last 9 sts, K9—72 sts.
Row 27: K3, [K2, K2tog, K2] to last 3 sts, K3—61 sts.
Row 33: K3, [K1, K2tog, K2] to last 3 sts, K3—50 sts.
Row 37: K3, [K1, K2tog, K1] to last 3 sts, K3—39 sts.
Rows 39–41: K. BO neck edge k-wise. Sew BO edge of cardigan to neck edge.

ARMS (make 2)

With C, CO 6 for shoulder.

Rows 1–2, 16–27: St st.
Rows 3–12: St st, inc 1 st at beg of each row—16 sts.
Rows 13–15: St st, CO 2 at beg of each row—20 sts. Pm at each end of row.

ELBOW

Row 16 (RS): K15, yf, sl 1, yb, turn.
Rows 17, 25: Sl 1, P10, yb, sl 1, yf, turn.
Rows 18, 24: Sl 1, K8, yf, sl 1, yb, turn.
Rows 19, 23: Sl 1, P6, yb, sl 1, yf, turn.

Rows 20, 22: Sl 1, K4, yf, sl 1, yb, turn.
Row 21: Sl 1, P2, yb, sl 1, yf, turn.
Row 26: Sl 1, K across.
Rows 27–29, 31–35, 37–39: St st.
Row 30: [K1, K2tog, K1] across—15 sts.
Row 36: K3, [K2tog, K4] 2 times—13 sts.
Rows 40–43: K for cuff.

HAND

Rows 44–45: With B, St st.
Row 46: K1, [Kfb, K2] across—17 sts.
Row 47: P.

THUMB

Rows 48–49: St st, CO 4 sts at beg of each row—25 sts.
Rows 50–51, 54–57: St st.
Rows 52–53: St st, BO 4 sts at beg of each row—17 sts.
Row 58: [K1, K2tog] to last 2 sts, K2—12 sts.
Row 59: P.
Row 60: K2tog across—6 sts.

Cut yarn leaving a long tail, thread tail through rem sts, gather tightly and fasten off. Sew ends of rows tog on hand and sleeve to markers, stuff firmly. Sew CO sts of each sleeve in line with neck edge of cardigan, making sure to sew through cardigan and body at the same time. Add more stuffing in tops of sleeves as necessary.

BASKET

BASE

With F, CO 12 sts.

Rows 1–2: [K2, P2] across.
Rows 3–4: [P2, K2] across.
Rows 5–28: Repeat last 4 rows 6 times, BO.

SIDES

With F, CO 60 sts.

Rows 1–2: [K2, P2] across.
Rows 3–4: [P2, K2] across.
Rows 5–16: Rep last 4 rows 3 times.

Sew ends of rows tog. Sew CO edge of sides to outer edges of base.

HANDLE

With F, CO 8, K 60 rows, BO.

Fold handle in half lengthways and slip stitch in place. Sew CO and BO edges to inner edges of basket sides as illustrated. Place basket on left arm.

CARROTS (make 3)

With F, CO 10 for top edge.

Row 1 (RS): P.
Row 2: With E, Kfb in each st across—20 sts.
Rows 3–11, 13–21, 23–29, 31–35: Rev St st.
Row 12: [K3, K2tog] across—16 sts.
Row 22: [K2, K2tog] across—12 sts.
Row 30: [K1, K2tog] across—8 sts.
Row 36: K2tog across—4 sts.

Cut yarn leaving a long tail, thread tail through rem sts, gather tightly and fasten off. Tightly gather CO sts and fasten off. Sew ends of rows tog, stuffing firmly before closing seam. With G, work a small tassel and sew to center of CO edge. Place one carrot in the crook of right elbow and the rem two carrots in the basket.

FINISHING

Weave in all ends.

Ollie the Octopus

Measurements

Height 5in/13cm

Materials

* Stylecraft Special DK 3.5oz/100g balls 100% Acrylic, one ball each: Turquoise 1068 (A), White 1001 (B), and Black 1002 (C)
* 3.5oz/100g Stuffing
* Stitch markers
* Knitting needles size US 2 (3mm)

Gauge

26 sts and 36 rows = 4in/10cm in St st.

BODY

With A, CO 12.

Rows 1–2, 8–10, 12–14: St st.
Row 3: Kfb in each st across—24 sts.
Rows 4, 6: P.
Row 5: [Kfb, K1] across—36 sts.
Row 7: [K1, Kfb, K1] across—48 sts.
Row 11: [K1, Kfb, K2] across—60 sts.
Row 15: [K2, Kfb, K2] across—72 sts.
Rows 16–48: St st, pm at center row 32.

TOP OF HEAD

Row 49: [K2, K2tog, K2] across—60 sts.
Row 50 and all WS rows: P.
Row 51: [K2, K2tog, K1] across—48 sts.
Row 53: [K1, K2tog, K1] across—36 sts.
Row 55: [K1, K2tog] across—24 sts.
Row 57: K2tog across—12 sts.

Cut yarn leaving a long tail, thread tail through rem sts, gather tightly and fasten off. Sew ends of rows tog, stuffing firmly before closing seam. Tightly gather CO edge and fasten off.

LEGS (make 8)

With A, CO 79.

Rows 1–2: St st.
Row 3: K61, yf, sl 1, yb, turn, leaving rem sts unworked.
Row 4 and foll WS rows: Sl 1, P across.
Row 5: K41, yf, sl 1, yb, turn.
Row 7: K25, yf, sl 1, yb, turn.
Row 9: K18, yf, sl 1, yb, turn.
Row 11: K13, yf, sl 1, yb, turn.
Row 12 and foll WS rows: With B, sl 1, K across.
Row 13: K14, yf, sl 1, yb, turn.
Row 15: K19, yf, sl 1, yb, turn.
Row 17: K26, yf, sl 1, yb, turn.
Row 19: K42, yf, sl 1, yb, turn.
Row 21: K62, yf, sl 1, yb, turn.
Rows 23–24: K all sts, BO.

Starting at tip, with RS out whip st CO and BO edges tog, pulling tight every 5–8 sts to curl the ends of the legs for 4–5.5in/10–13cms, cont so the top section remains straight. Stuff the top section of the leg firmly. Sew legs evenly spaced around the lower edge of body at row 15, making sure the octopus can sit.

NOSE

With A, embroider several straight sts over marked sts in row 32.
the center 2 sts and 6 knitted rows above the base of mouth.

MOUTH

With C, embroider a "V" of two long sts worked out from st 6 rows below nose.

EYES (make 2)

With B, CO 12.

Rows 1–4: St st.
Row 5: With C, K2tog across—6 sts.

Cut yarn leaving a long tail, thread tail through rem sts, gather tightly and fasten off. Sew ends of rows tog and stuff firmly. Tightly gather CO edge and fasten off. With A, embroider a circle of 8 chain sts around C on each eye. With B, make a tiny straight stitch for the twinkle in each eye. Sew eyes 7 rows above the nose and 2 sts from center.

FINISHING

Weave in all ends.

Percy the Pig

Measurements

Height 14in/35cm

Materials

* Stylecraft Special DK 3.5oz/100g balls 100% Acrylic, one ball each: Candy Floss 1130 (A), Meadow 1065 (B), Royal 1117 (C), White 1001 (D), Camel 1420 (E), Matador 1010 (F), Walnut 1054 (G), Cloud Blue 1019 (H), Black 1002 (J), Turquoise 1068 (K), and Silver 1203 (L)
* 6.35oz/180g Stuffing
* Knitting needles size US 2 (3mm) and US 8 (5mm)
* Stitch holder
* Stitch markers
* Red-colored pencil
* Pieces of thick card stock for cake

Gauge

26 sts and 36 rows = 4in/10cm in St st with smaller needles.

NOTE: Use smaller needles throughout unless otherwise stated.

RIGHT LEG

SOLE

With J, CO 26.
Rows 1–2: St st.
Row 3 (RS): K1, Kfb in next 24 sts, K1—50 sts.
Rows 4–5: St st, cut J.

UPPER

Rows 6–16: With G, St st.

SHAPE TOP OF SHOE

Row 17: K6, K2tog 13 times, K18—37 sts.
Row 18: P.
Row 19: K6, K2tog 7 times, K17—30 sts.
Rows 20–22: G st, cut G.

LEG

Rows 23–58: With B, St st. Cut yarn, slip 30 sts onto holder.

LEFT LEG

Rep rows 1–16 of right leg.

SHAPE TOP OF SHOE

Row 17: K18, K2tog 13 times, K6—37 sts.
Row 18: P.
Row 19: K17, K2tog 7 times, K6—30 sts.
Rows 20–22: G st color G, cut G.

LEG

Rows 23–58: With B, St st. Do not break off yarn.

JOINING LEGS

Row 59 (RS): With B and RS facing, K30 sts of left leg, K30 sts of right leg—60 sts.
Rows 60–80: St st. Cut B.

BODY

Rows 81–98: With D, St st.

SHAPE SIDES

Row 99: K9, K2tog 6 times, K18, K2tog 6 times, K9—48 sts.
Rows 100–104: St st.

SHAPE NECK

Row 105: [K1, K2tog, K1] across—36 sts.
Row 106: P.
Row 107: [K1, K2tog] across—24 sts.
Row 108: P, cut D.

NECK

Rows 109–114: With A, St st. BO for top of neck.

Sew row ends tog for each leg from joining row to base edge of sole. Fold sole and sew across CO edges of each foot. Sew ends of rows tog creating a seam down the back of the neck and body, stuffing firmly before closing seam.

HEAD

With A, CO 10 for neck edge.

Rows 1–2: St st.
Row 3: Kfb into every st across—20 sts.
Rows 4, 6, 8: P.
Row 5: [Kfb, K1] across—30 sts.
Row 7: [K1, Kfb, K1] across—40 sts.
Row 9: [K1, Kfb, K2] across—50 sts.
Row 10: P.

SHAPE SNOUT

Rows 11–18: CO 3 sts at beg of row. Pm at each end of row—74 sts.
Rows 19–20: St st.
Rows 21–22: Inc 1 st at each end row—78 sts.
Rows 23–30: St st. Pm at each end of last row.

SHAPE TOP OF SNOUT

Rows 31–32: BO 5 sts at beg of row—68 sts.
Rows 33–34: BO 4 sts at beg of row—60 sts.
Rows 35–36: BO 3 sts at beg of row—54 sts.
Rows 37–38: BO 2 sts at beg of row—50 sts.
Rows 39–40: St st.

SHAPE TOP OF HEAD

Row 41: [K3, K2tog] across—40 sts.
Row 42 and foll WS rows: P.
Row 43: [K2, K2tog] across—30 sts.
Row 45: [K1, K2tog] across—20 sts.
Row 47: K2tog across—10 sts.

Cut yarn leaving a long tail, thread tail through rem sts, gather tightly and fasten off. Sew ends of rows tog from top of head to markers at top of snout. Sew row ends tog from next set of markers leaving a gap next to CO edge.

SNOUT

With A, CO 6.

Row 1: P.
Rows 2–3: Inc 1 st at each end of row—10 sts.
Rows 4–9: St st.
Rows 10–11: Dec 1 st at each end of row—6 sts. BO.

Sew snout piece into opening bet markers on head. Stuff head firmly and close seam. Gather CO sts of head, pull up tightly and fasten off. With J, work two small stitches for nostrils.

EYES (make 2)

With D, CO 12.

Rows 1–4: St st, cut D.
Row 5: With J, K2tog across—6 sts.

Cut yarn leaving a long tail, thread tail through rem sts, gather tightly and fasten off. Sew ends of rows tog, stuff firmly. Gather CO sts, pull up tightly and fasten off. With K, work a circle of 8 chain sts around J on each eye. With D work a tiny straight stitch for twinkle in each eye. Sew eyes just above the snout.

EARS (make 2)

With A, CO 14.
Rows 1–2: St st.
Row 3 (RS): Kfb into every st across—28 sts.
Rows 4–8: St st.

SHAPE TOP OF EAR

Rows 9–26: Dec 1 st at beg of row—10 sts.
Row 27: K2tog across—5 sts.

Cut yarn leaving a long tail, thread tail through rem sts, gather tightly and fasten off. Sew ends of rows tog and across CO edge. With the seam at outer edge, sew ears to either side of head 4 rows above cheeks. Fold the top over and sew in place. (See photograph on p. 55.)

CHEEKS

With a red-colored pencil, slightly wet the lead and gently color cheeks working in a circular motion.

ARMS (make 2)

SLEEVE

With D, CO 8.

Rows 1–2: St st.
Row 3: K1, Kfb 6 times, K1—14 sts.
Row 4: P.
Rows 5–14: Inc 1 st at each end of row—24 sts.
Rows 15–16: CO 2 sts at each end of row. Pm at each end of last row—28 sts.
Rows 17–20: St st.

CUFF

Rows 21–22: G st. Cut D.

ARM

Rows 23–34: With A, St st.

SHAPE ARM

Row 35: [K1, K2tog, K1] across—21 sts.
Rows 36–50: St st.
Row 51: [K1, K2tog] across—14 sts.
Rows 52–56: St st.
Row 57: K2tog across—7 sts.

Cut yarn leaving a long tail, thread tail through rem sts, gather tightly and fasten off.

SWEATER

BACK AND FRONT (make 2)

With C, CO 55.

Row 1 (RS): K1, [P1, K1] across.
Row 2: P1, [K1, P1] across.
Rows 3–4: Rep row 1–2.
Rows 5-12: St st.
Row 13: Dec 1 st at each end of row.
Rows 14–25: Rep row 11–13—35 sts.
Rows 26–37: St st.

SHAPE SHOULDERS

Rows 38–39: BO 7 sts at beg of row, St st—21 sts.

NECKBAND

Rows 40–43: Rep row 1–4. BO loosely in rib with larger needles.

SLEEVES (make 2)

With C, CO 27.

Row 1 (RS): K1, [P1, K1] across.
Row 2: P1, [K1, P1] across.
Rows 3–8: St st.
Row 9: St st, inc 1 st at each end of row—29 sts.
Rows 10–15: Rep row 4-9—31 sts.
Rows 16–24: St st. BO loosely.

FINISHING

Sew shoulder and neckband seams. Match center of sleeve with shoulder seam, sew in sleeves. Sew side and sleeve seams. Place sweater on pig.

NAPKIN/BIB

With D, CO 3.

Rows 1–30: G st, inc 1 st at beg of each row—33 sts.

TIES

Rows 31–32: CO 40 sts at beg of row—113 sts.
Rows 33–34: BO 40 sts at beg of row—33 sts.
Row 35: BO. Weave in ends. Tie at back of neck.

PLATE

With two strands of H held together, CO 80. Cut one strand and cont.

Rows 1–2: P.
Row 3: [K6, K2tog] across—70 sts.
Row 4 and all WS rows: P.
Row 5: [K5, K2tog] across—60 sts.
Row 7: [K4, K2tog] across—50 sts.
Row 9: [K3, K2tog] across—40 sts.
Row 11: [K2, K2tog] across—30 sts.
Row 13: [K1, K2tog] across—20 sts.
Row 15: K2tog across—10 sts.

Cut yarn leaving a long tail, thread tail through rem sts, gather tightly and fasten off. Sew ends of rows tog.

CAKE

With E, CO 10.

Row 1: K.
Row 2 and foll WS rows: P.
Row 3: Kfb in each st across—20 sts.
Row 5: [Kfb, K1] across—30 sts.
Row 7: [K1, Kfb, K1] across—40 sts.
Row 9: [K1, Kfb, K2] across—50 sts.
Row 11: [K2, Kfb, K2] across—60 sts.
Rows 13–14: K for outer edge of base.
Rows 15–19: St st.
Row 20: With D, P.
Rows 21–23: Rev St st.
Rows 24–27: With E, St st.
Rows 28–35: Rep Rows 20–27.
Row 36: With D, P.
Rows 37–39: Rev St st.
Row 40: [K4, K2tog] across—50 sts.
Row 41 and foll RS rows: P.
Row 42: [K3, K2tog] across—40 sts.
Row 44: [K2, K2tog] across—30 sts.
Row 46: [K1, K2tog] across—20 sts.
Row 48: K2tog across—10 sts.

Cut yarn leaving a long tail, thread tail through rem sts, gather tightly and fasten off. Sew ends of rows tog leaving base open. Cut a circle of cardboard and place inside at the base. Stuff firmly and close base, tightly gathering CO sts, and fasten off.

CHERRIES (make 5)

With F, CO 4.

Row 1 (WS): Kfb in each st across—8 sts.
Rows 2–4: St st.
Row 5: K2tog across—4 sts.

Cut yarn leaving a long tail, thread tail through rem sts, gather tightly and fasten off. Sew ends of rows tog, stuff, tighly gather CO sts, and fasten off. Sew cherries on top of cake.

SPOON

With L, CO 5.
Row 1: Kfb 4 times, K1—9 sts.
Rows 2–32: St st.

Cut yarn leaving a long tail, thread tail through rem sts, gather tightly and fasten off. Seam handle. Trace shape of spoon on thick cardboard, cut out. Place cardboard in spoon and close seam. Sew spoon to right hoof.

FINISHING

Weave in all ends.

Primrose the Nighttime Teddy

BODY

With A, CO 12.

Row 1: K.
Row 2 and all WS rows: P.
Row 3: Kfb in each st across—24 sts.
Row 5: [Kfb, K1] across—36 sts.
Row 7: [K1, Kfb, K1] across—48 sts.
Row 9: [K1, Kfb, K2] across—60 sts.

TUMMY

Row 11: K28, Kfb, K2, Kfb, K28—62 sts.
Row 13: K29, Kfb, K2, Kfb, K29—64 sts.
Row 15: K30, Kfb, K2, Kfb, K30—66 sts.
Row 17: K31, Kfb, K2, Kfb, K31—68 sts.
Row 19: K32, Kfb, K2, Kfb, K32—70 sts.
Row 21: K33, Kfb, K2, Kfb, K33—72 sts.
Rows 22–36: St st.
Row 37: K34, K2tog, skp, K34—70 sts.
Row 39: K33, K2tog, skp, K33—68 sts.
Row 41: K32, K2tog, skp, K32—66 sts.
Row 43: K31, K2tog, skp, K31—64 sts.
Row 45: K30, K2tog, skp, K30—62 sts.

Row 47: K29, K2tog, skp, K29—60 sts.
Row 49: K.

SIDES OF BODY

Row 51: [K2, K2tog, K2] across—50 sts.
Row 53: K.
Row 55: [K2, K2tog, K1] across—40 sts.

SHOULDERS

Row 57: K6, K2tog 4 times, K12, K2tog 4 times, K6—32 sts.
Rows 58–60: St st, BO.

Sew ends of rows tog, stuff firmly. Tightly gather CO sts and fasten off.

HEAD

With A, CO 12.

Row 1: K.
Row 2 and all WS rows: P.
Row 3: Kfb in each st across—24 sts.
Row 5: K7, Kfb, pm, K8, pm, Kfb, K7—26 sts.
Rows 7–13: St st, inc before 1st marker (m) and after 2nd on RS rows—34 sts.

FACE

Row 15: Kfb, [K1, Kfb] 6 times, K8, Kfb, [K1, Kfb] 6 times—48 sts.
Row 17: K16, Kfb, pm, K2, pm, Kfb, K8, Kfb, pm, K2, pm, Kfb, K16—52 sts.
Pm through center sts for eye position.
Rows 19–27: K to m, Kfb, K2, Kfb, K to m, Kfb, K2, Kfb, K to end—72 sts.
Row 29: K2, [Kfb, K3] 5 times, Kfb, K2, Kfb, K20, Kfb, K2, Kfb, [K3, Kfb] 5 times, K2—86 sts. Pm for ear position 8 sts from center on each side.
Rows 30–44: St st.

BACK OF HEAD

Row 45: K1, [K2, K2tog, K2] to last st, K1—72 sts.
Row 47: K1, [K1, K2tog, K2] to last st, K1—58 sts.
Row 49: K1, [K1, K2tog, K1] to last st, K1—44 sts.
Row 51: K1, [K2tog, K1] to last st, K1—30 sts.
Row 53: K2tog across—15 sts.

Cut yarn leaving a long tail, thread tail through rem sts, gather tightly and fasten off. Tightly gather CO sts and fasten off. Sew ends of rows tog, stuffing body firmly before closing seam. This seam will run underneath the head. Sew head to top of neck opening as illustrated. With G, embroider a circle of 5 chain sts for each eye, 3 sts to either side of marker.

NOSE

With H, CO 10.

Rows 1–2: St st.
Rows 3–6: St st, dec 1 st at each end of row—2 sts.
Row 7: K2tog, cut yarn leaving a long tail and fasten off. Sew nose to snout as illustrated. With G, embroider mouth.

EARS (make 2 with A for outer and 2 with F for inner)

With A, CO 14 sts.

Rows 1–6: St st.
Rows 7–10: St st, dec 1 st at each end of row—6 sts. BO.

Sew edges of outer and inner ear in pairs. Sew CO edge of ears in a slightly curved shape to the outside of the markers in row 29 of head.

ARMS

RIGHT ARM

With A, CO 14.

Rows 1–2, 4–8, 11–22, 24–32, 34–36: St st.
Row 3: [Kfb, K1] across—21 sts.
Rows 9–10: CO 2 sts at beg of row, St st—25 sts. Pm at each end of last row.
Row 23: [K5, K2tog] 3 times, K4—22 sts.
Row 33: K6, [K2tog, K6] 2 times—20 sts.

PAW

1ST SIDE

Row 37: K9, Kfb and turn.
Rows 38–40: Working on 11 sts only, St st.
Rows 41–46: St st, dec 1 st at beg of each row—5 sts. BO.

2ND SIDE

With RS facing, join F to row 37 and work across rem 10 sts, Kfb, K9—11 sts. Rep rows 38–46 of 1st side.

Left Arm Rep rows 1–36 of right arm.

Paw Rep as rows 37–46 of right arm, joining F for 1st side and A for 2nd side. Sew around paw. Sew ends of rows tog to markers leaving top edge open. Stuff firmly and sew to top of body.

LEGS (make 2)

With A, CO 46.

Rows 1–10: St st.
Row 11: K13, K2tog 10 times, K13—36 sts.
Row 12: P.

Row 13: K12, K2tog 6 times, K12—30 sts.
Row 14: P, pm at center front.
Row 15: K10, BO 10 sts for top of foot, K to end—20 sts.
Rows 16–22: St st, working across all sts—20 sts.
Row 23: [K2, Kfb, K2] across—24 sts.
Rows 24–28, 30–34, 36–42: St st.
Row 29: [K2, Kfb, K3] across—28 sts.
Row 35: [K3, Kfb, K3] across—32 sts.
Row 43: K1, [skp, K11, K2tog] 2 times, K1—28 sts.
Rows 44, 46, 48: P.
Row 45: K1, [skp, K9, K2tog] 2 times, K1—24 sts.
Row 47: K1, [skp, K7, K2tog] 2 times, K1—20 sts.
Row 49: K1, [skp, K5, K2tog] 2 times, K1—16 sts.
Row 50: P. BO.

Sew ends of rows tog from foot to hip leaving a 1in/2.5cm gap at top. Fold BO sts in row 15 in half using marker as a guide and sew BO edges tog at top of foot.

SOLES (make 2)

With B, CO 6.

Rows 1–2, 5–16: St st.
Rows 3–4: St st, inc 1 st at each end of row—10 sts.
Rows 17–18: St st, dec 1 st at each end of row—6 sts. BO.

Sew sole to CO edge of leg, stuff leg firmly. Sew legs to lower edge of body as illustrated.

NIGHTGOWN

FRONT

With C, CO 67.

Rows 1–4, 6–8, 70–72, 80–84: St st.
Row 5 (Picot): K1, [yo, K2tog] across.
Rows 9–12: With D, K.
Rows 13–16: With B, St st.
Row 17: St st, dec 1 st at each end of row—65 sts.
Rows 18–69: St st, [dec 1 st at each end of every 4th row] 13 times—39 sts.

ARMHOLES

Rows 73–74: BO off 3 sts at beg of row, St st—33 sts.
Rows 75–79: St st, dec 1 st at each end of row—23 sts.

NECK

Row 85: K6, K2tog, BO 7 sts, skp, K to end.
Rows 86–89: Join a 2nd end of B to work both sides at the same time. St st, dec 1 st at each side of neck edge—3 sts. BO.

BACK

Rep row 1–84 of front. Work 5 rows even in St st, BO, sew shoulder seams.

SLEEVES

With C, CO 23.

Rows 1–2, 4–6: St st.
Row 3 (Picot): K1, [yo, K2tog] across.
Rows 7, 8, 10: With D, K.
Row 9: K, inc 1 st at each end of row—25 sts.
Rows 11–14, 16–18, 20–22: With B, St st.
Rows 15, 19: St st, inc 1 st at each end of row—29 sts.

SLEEVE CAP

Rows 23–24: St st, BO 3 sts at beg of row—23 sts.
Rows 25–29: St st, dec 1 st at each end of row—13 sts.
Row 30: P. BO.

Sew with center of BO edge of sleeve at shoulder seam. Sew side and sleeve seams. Fold CO edge to WS at picot row to form frills, slip stitch to WS.

BUTTON BAND

With B, CO 22, K1 row, BO.
With C, embroider 5 evenly spaced small French knots for buttons as illustrated. Sew button band to center front.

NIGHT HAT

Stripe patt: 2 rows B, 2 rows C.

With C, CO 59.

Rows 1–4, 6–9: St st.
Row 5 (Picot): K1, [yo, K2tog] across.
Rows 10–13: With D, K, inc 1 st at center of last row—60 sts.
Beg Stripe patt.
Rows 14–22, 24–34, 36–46, 48–58, 60–68, 70–76: St st.
Row 23: [K4, K2tog] across—50 sts.
Row 35: [K3, K2tog] across—40 sts.
Row 47: [K2, K2tog] across—30 sts.
Row 59: [K1, K2tog] across—20 sts.
Row 69: K2tog across—10 sts.
Row 77: K2tog across—5 sts.
Rows 78–82: St st.

Cut yarn leaving a long tail, thread tail through rem sts, gather tightly and fasten off. Sew row ends tog. Fold CO edge to WS at picot row to form frills, slip stitch to WS. With D, make a small tassel and sew to end of hat. Sew hat on teddy at an angle covering one ear as pictured on page 63.

HOT WATER BOTTLE

BOTTLE (make 2)

With E, CO 13.
Row 1: Kfb, K to last st, Kfb—15 sts.
Row 2: K2, P to last 2 sts, K2.
Rows 3–6: Rep rows 1–2 two times—19 sts.
Rows 7–26: St st, K 1st 2 and last 2 sts on WS rows.
Row 27: Skp, K to last 2 sts, K2tog—17 sts.
Row 28: K2, P to last 2 sts, K2.
Rows 29–32: Rep rows 27–28 2 times—13 sts. BO.
With RS out, whip st around pieces, stuffing lightly to keep the shape flat.

STOPPER

With C, CO 5, K 10 rows, BO.

Roll strip tightly and sew ends. Sew one end of stopper to top of bottle.

BOTTLE NECK

With E, CO 18.

Rows 1–2: K.
Rows 3–5: St st.
Row 6: [P1, P2tog] across—12 sts, BO.

Sew ends of rows tog, sew BO edge just below the base of the stopper as illustrated. Place the finished hot water bottle underneath Primrose's left arm and sew in place.

FINISHING

Weave in all ends.

Rio the Fish

Measurements

Length 13in/33cm, Height 5in/13cm

Materials

* Stylecraft Special DK 3.5oz/100g balls 100% Acrylic, one ball each:
  Jaffa 1256 (A), Fiesta 1257 (B), White 1001 (C), Turquoise 1068 (D),
  and Black 1002 (E).
* 3.5oz/100g Stuffing
* Stitch markers
* Knitting needles size US 2 (3mm), 2 pairs

Gauge

26 sts and 36 rows = 4in/10cm in St st.

Note: Body is worked with one set of needles and the scales are worked
with the second. The pieces are joined as the work progresses.

WORK 1ST SET OF SCALES

With B, CO 45.

Row 1: (RS) 1/1 rib.
Row 2: P3tog, [K3tog, P3tog] across—15 sts. Do not cut yarn.

BODY

With A and 2nd pair of needles, CO 8.

Rows 1–2: St st.
Row 3: (RS) K1, Kfb 7 times—15 sts.
Rows 4–10: St st.

Join scales to body

Row 11: With WS of scales facing RS of body, using B, K each scale st with the corresponding body st to join the pieces—15 sts.
Row 12: P.
Row 13: Kfb into each st across—30 sts.
Rows 14–20: St st. Cut yarn and set aside.

WORK 2ND SET OF SCALES

With A, CO 90.

Row 1 (RS): 1/1 rib.
Row 2: [K3tog, P3tog] across—30 sts. Do not cut yarn.

Join 2nd set of scales

Rows 21–22: With A, rep rows 11–12—30 sts.
Row 23: [Kfb, K1] across—45 sts.
Rows 24–30: St st. Cut yarn and set aside.

WORK 3RD SET OF SCALES

With B, CO 135 sts.

Row 1: (RS) 1/1 rib.
Row 2: P3tog, [K3tog, P3tog] across—45 sts. Do not cut yarn.

Join 3rd set of scales

Rows 31–32: With B, rep rows 11–12—45 sts.
Row 33: [K1, Kfb, K1] across—60 sts.
Rows 34–40: St st. Cut yarn and set aside.

WORK 4TH SET OF SCALES

With A, CO 180 sts.

Row 1: (RS) 1/1 rib.
Row 2: [K3tog, P3tog] across—60 sts. Do not cut yarn.

Join 4th set of scales

Rows 41–42: With A, rep rows 11–12—60 sts.
Row 43: [K1, Kfb, K2] across—75 sts.
Rows 44–50: St st. Cut yarn and set aside.

WORK 5TH SET OF SCALES

With B, CO 225 sts.

Row 1: (RS) 1/1 rib.
Row 2: P3tog, [K3tog, P3tog] across—75 sts. Do not cut yarn.

Join 5th set of scales

Row 51–52: With A, rep rows 11–12—75 sts.
Row 53: [K2, Kfb, K2] across—90 sts.
Row 54–60: St st. Cut yarn and set aside.

WORK 6TH SET OF SCALES

With A, CO 270 sts.

Row 1: (RS) 1/1 rib.
Row 2: [K3tog, P3tog] across—90 sts. Do not cut yarn.

Join 6th set of scales

Row 51: With A, rep row 11—90 sts.

HEAD

Row 52: K.
Rows 53–58, 60–62, 64–66, 68–70, 72–74, 76–78, 80–82, 84–86: St st.
Row 59: [K4, K2tog, K3] across—80 sts.
Row 63: [K3, K2tog, K3] across—70 sts. Pm for eye placement.
Row 67: [K3, K2tog, K2] across—60 sts.
Row 71: [K2, K2tog, K2] across—50 sts.
Row 75: [K2, K2tog, K1] across—40 sts.
Row 79: [K1, K2tog, K1] across—30 sts.
Row 83: [K1, K2tog] across—20 sts.
Row 87: K2tog across—10 sts.

Cut yarn leaving a long tail, thread tail through rem sts, gather tightly and fasten off. Tightly gather CO sts and fasten off. Sew ends of rows tog on body and head, stuffing body firmly before closing seam. This seam will run underneath the fish. Place the fish on its side and flatten into shape.

EYES (make 2)

With C, CO 12.

Rows 1–4: St st.
Row 5: With E, K2tog across—6 sts.

Cut yarn leaving a long tail, thread tail through rem sts, gather tightly and fasten off. Sew ends of rows tog and stuff firmly. Tightly gather CO sts and fasten off. With D, embroider a circle of 8 chain sts around C on each eye. With C, make a tiny straight stitch for the twinkle in each eye. Sew eyes as marked.

TAIL

FIRST SIDE

With B, CO 5.

Row 1: Kfb in each st across —10 sts.
Rows 2–4: St st.
Rows 5–24: St st, inc 1 st at beg of each row—30 sts.

Cut yarn and leave sts on a needle.

SECOND SIDE

With the other needles, rep first side, do not cut yarn.

Row 25: (Joining) K 30 sts from second side, then 30 sts from first side—60 sts. Pm at each end of row.
Row 26: P.

BASE OF TAIL

Row 27: [K1, K2tog, K1] across—45 sts.
Rows 28, 30: P.
Row 29: [K1, K2tog] across—30 sts.
Row 31: K2tog across—15 sts.
Rows 32–34: St st. BO.

Sew row ends tog from BO to marker, sew each side of tail tog. Do not stuff. Sew BO edge of tail to CO edge of body.

FINS (make 2)

With B, CO 10.

Rows 1–2, 4, 6–8: St st.
Row 3: Kfb in each st across—20 sts.
Row 4: P.
Row 5: [Kfb, K1] across—30 sts.
Rows 9–28: St st, dec 1 st at beg of each row—10 sts.
Row 29: K2tog across—5 sts.

Cut yarn leaving a long tail, thread tail through rem sts, gather tightly and fasten off. Sew ends of rows tog. Lay flat with seam at back and sew CO edge to side of body over 5th set of scales.

LIPS

With B, CO 15.

Row 1: K1, [Kfb, K1] across—22 sts.
Rows 2–4: St st.
Row 5: K1, [K2tog, K1] across—15 sts. BO k-wise.
Sew row ends tog to form a circle. Whip st CO and BO edges tog. Fold edges lengthways and whip st to last row of face.

FINISHING

Weave in all ends.

Rosie the Dolly

Measurements

Height 16in/41cm (standing), 11in/28cm (sitting)

Materials

* Stylecraft Special DK 3.5oz/100g balls 100% Acrylic, one ball each: Walnut 1054 (A), Magenta 1084 (B), Soft Peach 1240 (C), Citron 1263 (D), Sunshine 1114 (E), Lipstick 1246 (F), Pomegranate 1083 (G), Raspberry 1023 (H), and Dark Brown 1004 (I)
* 6.5oz/185g Stuffing
* Stitch markers
* Red-colored pencil
* Crochet hook size US 1.5 (2.5mm)
* Knitting needles size US 2 (3mm)

Gauge

26 sts and 36 rows = 4in/10cm in St st.

BODY

Stripe Patt: 2 rows D, 2 rows E.

LOWER BODY

With D, CO 48, pm in center st.

Rows 1–4: Beg Stripe Patt, St st.
Row 5: K9, Kfb 6 times, K18, Kfb 6 times, K9—60 sts.
Rows 6–26: St st.

UPPER BODY

Rows 27–44: With B, St st.

SIDES

Row 45: K9, K2tog 6 times, K18, K2tog 6 times, K9—48 sts.
Rows 46–50: St st.

NECK

Row 51: [K1, K2tog, K1] across—36 sts.

HEAD

Rows 52–54: With C, St st, pm for neck.
Row 55: K1, Kfb 34 times, K1—70 sts.
Rows 56–82: St st, pm in center st of row 79 and last st of row 63 for hair. Pm in center of row 67 for eyes.

TOP OF HEAD

Row 83: [K5, K2tog] across—60 sts.
Row 84 and all WS rows: P.
Row 85: [K4, K2tog] across—50 sts.
Row 87: [K3, K2tog] across—40 sts.
Row 89: [K2, K2tog] across—30 sts.
Row 91: [K1, K2tog] across—20 sts.
Row 93: K2tog across—10 sts.

Cut yarn leaving a long tail, thread tail through rem sts, gather tightly and fasten off. Sew ends of rows tog on body and head, stuffing firmly. Match center back seam with marker in CO edge, whip st closed. With C doubled, tightly gather every st of neck, fasten off.

SHOES & LEGS (make 2)

With A, CO 26 for sole.

Rows 1–2, 4, 5: St st.
Row 3: K1, Kfb 24 times, K1—50 sts.

SHOE UPPER

Rows 6–16: With G, St st.
Row 17: K11, K2tog 14 times, K11—36 sts.
Row 18: P.
Row 19: K10, K2tog 8 times, K10—28 sts.
Rows 20–22: K. Cut G.

LEG

Rows 23–58: Beg Stripe patt, St st.
Row 59: K3, K2tog 4 times, K6, K2tog 4 times, K3—20 sts.
Row 60: P, BO, pm in center st.

Fold each foot in half and whip st CO edge, sew ends of rows tog matching stripes, stuff firmly. Match center back seam to marker in BO edge, whip st across BO edge. Sew BO edges to CO edge of body with all vertical seams toward back of doll.

HAIR CAP

With A, CO 70.

Rows 1–22: K.
Row 23: [K5, K2tog] across—60 sts.
Row 24 and all WS rows: K.
Row 25: [K4, K2tog] across—50 sts.

Row 27: [K3, K2tog] across—40 sts.
Row 29: [K2, K2tog] across—30 sts.
Row 31: [K1, K2tog] across—20 sts.
Row 33: K2tog across—10 sts.

Cut yarn leaving a long tail, thread tail through rem sts, gather tightly and fasten off. Sew ends of rows tog. Backstitch cap to top of head with front and back edges at markers. Cut 16.5in/42cm lengths of A for hair. Use crochet hook to loop strands through cap until head is covered. Style and trim to neaten.

FACE

With I, embroider 4 straight stitches for each eye, making each eye 4 rows high, 4 sts apart at marker. With C, embroider several horizontal straight stitches over center 2 stitches 3 rows below eye marker. With H, embroider a 'V' of two stitches worked out from center, 3 rows below nose as illustrated. Using a red pencil, slightly wet the end and working in a circular motion shade in the cheeks as pictured and then slightly on the nose.

ARMS (make 2)

With B, CO 8 sts for shoulder.

Rows 1–2: St st.
Row 3: K1, Kfb 6 times, K1—14 sts.
Row 4: P.
Rows 5–14: St st, inc 1 st at beg of each row—24 sts.
Rows 15–16: St st, CO 2 sts at beg of each row—28 sts.
Rows 17–20: St st, pm at each end of row 17.
Rows 21–22: With F, K for cuff.

LOWER ARM

Rows 23–34: With C, St st.
Row 35: [K1, K2tog, K1] across—21 sts.
Rows 36–46: St st.

WRIST

Row 47: [K1, K2tog] across—14 sts.
Rows 48–50: St st.

HAND

Rows 51–52: St st, CO 6 sts at beg of each row for thumb—26 sts.
Rows 53–54: St st.
Rows 55–56: St st, BO 4 sts at beg of each row—18 sts.

FINGERS

Row 57: K2, Kfb, [K1, Kfb] 2 times, K3, Kfb, turn, leaving rem 3 sts unworked.

LITTLE FINGER

Row 58: P6, turn.
Rows 59–62: Working on 6 sts only, St st.

Cut yarn leaving a long tail, thread tail through rem sts, gather tightly and fasten off. Sew ends of rows 58–62 tog.

RING FINGER

Row 58: With RS facing and 9 sts on right needle, join C, K1, Kfb, from left needle, turn—12 sts.
Row 59: P6, turn.
Rows 60–65: Working on 6 sts only, St st.

Cut yarn leaving a long tail, thread tail through rem sts, gather tightly and fasten off. Sew ends of rows 58–65 tog.

MIDDLE FINGER

Row 58: With RS facing and 6 sts on right needle, join C, K1, Kfb, from left needle, turn—9 sts.
Row 59: P6, turn.
Rows 60–66: Working on 6 sts only, St st.

Cut yarn leaving a long tail, thread tail through rem sts, gather tightly and fasten off. Sew ends of rows 58–66 tog.

INDEX FINGER

Row 58: With RS facing and 3 sts on right needle, join C, K 3 sts from left needle—6 sts.
Rows 59–64: St st.

Cut yarn leaving a long tail, thread tail through rem sts, gather tightly and fasten off. Sew ends of rows 58–64 tog and around thumb. Sew ends of rows of hand and arm to markers. Stuff arm and hand firmly, omitting thumb and fingers. Sew CO edges of arms to side of body in line with last row of B on upper body.

SKIRT

With F, CO 156.

Rows 1–5: St st.
Row 6: K, for hem fold line.
Rows 7–18: With B, St st.
Row 19: [K6, P1, K6] across. **Note:** P1 marks position of roses.
Rows 20–44, 46–50, 52–54: St st.
Row 45: [K2, K2tog, K2] across—130 sts.
Row 51: [K2, K2tog, K1] across—104 sts.

WAIST

Row 55: K2, [K2tog, K1] across—70 sts. BO k-wise.

Sew ends of rows tog. Fold hem to wrong side and slip st in place. Sew BO edge to row 27 of body, matching seams at back of doll.

ROSES (make 13)

With F, CO 25.

Rows 1–3: St st.
Row 4: K1, [yo, K2tog] across.
Rows 5–7: St st. BO k-wise.

Sew CO and BO edges tog with RS out creating a picot edge. Roll strip lengthwise and sew into a rose-like shape. Sew through the base of rose to attach one each P st at lower edge of skirt. Sew last rose to center of body as illustrated.

FINISHING

Weave in all ends.

Ruby the Russian Doll

BODY

BASE

With A, CO 10.

Row 1: K.
Row 2 and all WS rows: P.
Row 3: Kfb in each st across—20 sts.
Row 5: [Kfb, K1] across—30 sts.
Row 7: [K1, Kfb, K1] across—40 sts.
Row 9: [K1, Kfb, K2] across—50 sts.
Row 11: [K2, Kfb, K2] across—60 sts.
Row 13: K1, Kfb, [K6, Kfb] to last st 2 sts, K2—69 sts.
Row 15: K.
Row 16: K, for fold line.
Rows 17–18: St st.

BODY DETAIL Work St st in intarsia method.

Row 19: K 22 A, 25 D, 22 A.
Row 20: P 22 A, 25 D, 22 A.
Rows 21–56: Rep last 2 rows 18 times.

SIDES OF BODY

Row 57: With A, K3, [K2tog, K5] 2 times, K2tog, K3. With D, K1, K2tog, [K5, K2tog] 3 times, K1. With A, K3, K2tog, [K5, K2tog] 2 times, K3—59 sts.
Row 58: P 19 A, 21 D, 19 A.
Row 59: K 19 A, 21 D, 19 A.
Row 60: P 19 A, 21 D, 19 A.
Row 61: With A, K1, [K2tog, K2] 4 times, K2tog. With D, [K1, K2tog] 7 times. With A, [K2tog, K2] 4 times, K2tog, K1—42 sts.
Row 62: P 14 A, 14 D, 14 A.
Row 63: K 14 A, 14 D, 14 A.
Row 64: P 14 A, 14 D, 14 A.

HEAD

Rows 65–66: With B, St st.
Row 67: [Kfb, K1] across—63 sts.
Row 68: P.

FACE DETAIL: Work St st in intarsia method.

Row 69: K 25 B, 13 C, 25 B.
Row 70: P 24 B, 15 C, 24 B.
Row 71: K 23 B, 17 C, 23 B.
Row 72: P 22 B, 19 C, 22 B.
Row 73: K 21 B, 21 C, 21 B.
Row 74: P 21 B, 21 C, 21 B.
Rows 75–82: Rep last 2 rows 4 times. Pm for eyes in center of row 80.
Row 83: K 21 B, 2 E, 17 C, 2 E, 21 B.
Row 84: P 21 B, 3 E, 15 C, 3 E, 21 B.
Row 85: K 22 B, 4 E, 11 C, 4 E, 22 B.
Row 86: P 23 B, 4 E, 9 C, 4 E, 23 B.
Row 87: K 24 B, 5 E, 5 C, 5 E, 24 B.
Row 88: P 25 B, 6 E, 1 C, 6 E, 25 B.
Row 89: K 26 B, 11 E, 26 B.
Row 90: P 27 B, 9 E, 27 B.
Row 91: K 28 B, 7 E, 28 B.
Row 92: P 30 B, 3 E, 30 B.
Rows 93–94: With B only, St st.

TOP OF HEAD

Row 95: [K3, K2tog, K2] across—54 sts.
Row 96 and foll WS rows: P.
Row 97: [K2, K2tog, K2] across—45 sts.
Row 99: [K1, K2tog, K2] across—36 sts.
Row 101: [K1, K2tog, K1] across—27 sts.
Row 103: [K1, K2tog] across—18 sts.
Row 104: P2tog across—9 sts.

Cut yarn leaving a long tail, thread tail through rem sts, gather tightly and fasten off. Tightly gather CO sts and fasten off. Sew ends of rows tog from base to fold line. Cut a 3.5in/9cm circle of thick cardboard, glue inside base, and allow to dry. Sew remainder of body and head seam, stuffing firmly before closing.

FACE

With F work a circle of 4 chains for each eye at marked row 5 sts apart. With E, split plies to embroider 3 tiny straight lines for eye lashes as illustrated. With C, embroider nose with 3 horizontal straight sts over center 3 stitches 3 rows below eyes. With H, embroider a "V" of 2 sts worked out from center 6 rows below nose as pictured. Using a red pencil, slightly wet the end and color cheeks as pictured, working in a circular motion and pressing lightly. With B, embroider a line of chain sts around face. With E, embroider a line of chain sts along the hair line that touches the face.

LACE COLLAR

With B, CO 4.

Row 1: K2, yo, K2—5 sts.
Rows 2, 4, 6: K.
Row 3: K3, yo, K2—6 sts.
Row 5: K2, yo, K2tog, yo, K2—7 sts.
Row 7: K3, yo, K2tog, yo, K2—8 sts.
Row 8: BO 4, K across—4 sts.
Rows 9–104: Rep rows 1–8. BO.

Sew CO and BO edges tog. Sew straight edge to row 65 of body, with the seam at center back of body.

ROSES (make 3)

With I, CO 21.

Rows 1–3: St st.
Row 4: K1 [yo, K2tog] across.
Rows 5–7: St st, BO k-wise for outer edge.

Sew CO and BO edges tog with RS out creating a picot edge. Roll strip lengthwise and sew into a rose-like shape. Sew through the base of rose onto the D section of body as illustrated.

SMALL FLOWERS (make 5 J & 5 L)

CO 10, K 1 row.

Cut yarn leaving a long tail, thread tail through rem sts, gather tightly and fasten off. Sew ends of rows tog. Sew flowers as illustrated. With N, embroider a small French knot in the center of each J flower and a French knot with O in the center of each L flower.

LARGE LEAVES (make 5)

With G, CO 7.

Row 1: K4, yf, sl 1, yb, turn.
Rows 2, 4: Sl 1, K across.
Row 3: K2, yf, sl 1, yb, turn.
Row 5: K across all 7 sts. BO.
Gather shorter row ends and fasten off. Sew leaves to roses as illustrated.

SMALL LEAVES (make 5)

With G, CO 5, BO. Sew leaves randomly over front of body section as illustrated.

VINES

With G, embroider several random wavy lines of chain st as illustrated.

FINISHING

Weave in all ends.

Rusty the Puppy

Measurements

Length 16in/41cm, Height 5in/12.5cm

Materials

* Stylecraft Special DK 3.5oz/100g balls 100% Acrylic, one ball each:
  Mocha 1064 (A), Cream 1005 (B), Petrol 1708 (C), Matador 1010 (D),
  White 1001 (E), Black 1002 (F), Walnut 1054 (G), and Saffron 1081 (H)
* 7oz/200g Stuffing
* Stitch markers
* Piece of thick cardboard
* Clear adhesive
* Knitting needles size US 2 (3mm)

Gauge

26 sts and 36 rows = 4in/10cm in St st.

BODY

With A, CO 12.

Rows 1–2, 6–8, 10–12, 14–18, 20–24, 26–42, 44–52, 54–62, 64–70, 72–76, 78–80: St st.
Row 3: Kfb in each st across—24 sts.
Row 4: P.
Row 5: [Kfb, K1] across—36 sts.
Row 9: [K1, Kfb, K1] across—48 sts.
Row 13: [K1, Kfb, K2] across—60 sts.
Row 19: [K2, Kfb, K2] across—72 sts.
Row 25: [K2, Kfb, K3] across—84 sts.
Row 43: [K2, K2tog, K3] across—72 sts.
Row 53: [K2, K2tog, K2] across—60 sts.
Row 63: [K1, K2tog, K2] across—48 sts.
Row 71: [K1, K2tog, K1] across—36 sts.
Row 77: [K1, K2tog] across—24 sts.
Row 81: K2tog across—12 sts.

Cut yarn leaving a long tail, thread tail through rem sts, gather tightly and fasten off. Tightly gather CO edge and fasten off. Sew ends of rows tog, creating a seam underneath body, stuffing body firmly before closing seam. Flatten into shape.

HEAD

With A, CO 12.

Rows 1–2, 8–10: St st.
Row 3: Kfb in each st across—24 sts.
Rows 4, 6, 12: P.
Row 5: [Kfb, K1] across—36 sts.
Row 7: [K1, Kfb, K1] across—48 sts.
Row 11: [K1, Kfb, K2] across—60 sts.
Rows 13–14, 16–18, 20–24, 26–30, 32–36, 38–52: With B, St st.
Row 15: K14, Kfb 2 times, pm, K28, Kfb 2 times, pm, K14—64 sts.
Rows 19, 25, 31, 37: K14, Kfb, K to 1 st before next marker, Kfb, K28, Kfb, K to 1 st before next marker, Kfb, K14—80 sts. Remove markers and pm in center sts.

MUZZLE

Row 53: [K3, K2tog, K3] across—70 sts. Pm for nose placement.
Row 54 and all WS rows: P.
Row 55: [K2, K2tog, K3] across—60 sts.
Row 57: [K2, K2tog, K2] across—50 sts.
Row 59: [K1, K2tog, K2] across—40 sts.
Row 61: [K1, K2tog, K1] across—30 sts.
Row 63: [K1, K2tog] across—20 sts.
Row 65: K2tog across—10 sts.

Cut yarn leaving a long tail, thread tail through rem sts, gather tightly and fasten off. Tightly gather CO edge and fasten off. Sew ends of rows tog, creating a seam down center back of head, stuffing firmly before closing. Flatten into shape. Lay body flat and sew head at a slight angle with the chin touching the surface.

NOSE

With G, CO 30.

Rows 1–4: St st.
Row 5: [K1, K2tog] across—20 sts.
Row 6: P.
Row 7: K2tog across—10 sts.
Row 8: P. BO. Pm at center.

Sew ends of rows tog. Match marker to seam and sew across BO edge. Stuff nose firmly and sew to muzzle aligning center lower edge with marked row.

EYES (make 2)

With E, CO 14.

Rows 1–4: St st.
Row 5: With F, K2tog across—7 sts.

Cut yarn leaving a long tail, thread tail through rem sts, gather tightly and fasten off. Tightly gather CO sts and fasten off. Sew ends of rows tog and stuff firmly. With G, embroider a circle of 8 chain sts around F on each eye. With E, make a tiny straight stitch for the twinkle in each eye. Sew eyes centered on face 4 sts apart, 10 rows above nose.

EYEBROWS

With G, embroider a slanted straight st as illustrated over each eye.

EARS (make 2 with A for outer ear and 2 with B for inner ear)

CO 12.

Rows 1–2, 9–52: St st.
Rows 3–8: St st, inc 1 st at beg of each row—18 sts.
Rows 53–58: St st, dec 1 st each end of each row—6 sts. BO.

Sew outer ear and inner ear tog, matching edges. Sew CO edge to top of head, just above color change, aligning center of each ear with inc at side of head.

FRONT LEGS (make 2)

With A, CO 20.

Rows 1–48: St st.
Row 49: Join B, K2A, [K1B, K2A] across. Cut A.

PAW

Row 50: With B, P.
Row 51: [Kfb, K1] across—30 sts.
Rows 52–60: St st.
Row 61: K4, K2tog 3 times, K10, K2tog 3 times, K4—24 sts.
Row 62: P. BO, pm in center st.

Sew ends of rows tog. Matching seam with marker, sew across BO edge, stuff firmly. With B doubled, stitch 2 indentations on paw as illustrated, make another st in each indentation with F. Sew CO edge of each leg to front edge of body 8 sts apart.

BACK LEGS (make 2)

With A, CO 20.

Rows 1–34: St st.
Rows 35–48: Rep rows 49–62 of front legs.

Finish same as front legs. Sew CO edge of each leg to back edge of body 14 sts apart.

TAIL

With A, CO 14.

Rows 1–6, 8–14, 16–22: St st.
Row 7: K2, [K2tog, K2] across—11 sts.
Row 15: K2, [K2tog, K1] across—8 sts.

TIP OF TAIL

Row 23: Join B, K2A, [K1B, K2A] across. Cut A.
Rows 24–26, 28–30: With B, St st.
Row 27: [K1, K2tog, K1] across—6 sts.
Row 31: [K1, K2tog] across—4 sts.
Row 32: P.

Cut yarn leaving a long tail, thread tail through rem sts, gather tightly and fasten off. Sew ends of rows tog and stuff firmly. Sew CO edge to lower edge of body as pictured on page 84.

COLLAR

With D, CO 6, K 80 rows, BO. Sew CO and BO edges to form a circle. Place on neck.

ID TAG

With H, CO 21.

Row 1: [K1, K2tog] across—14 sts.
Row 2: P.
Row 3: K2tog across—7 sts.

Cut yarn leaving a long tail, thread tail through rem sts, gather tightly and fasten off. Sew ends of rows tog. Sew to seam on collar.

BOWL

With C, CO 10 sts.

Row 1: K.
Row 2 and all WS rows: P.
Row 3: Kfb in each st across—20 sts.
Row 5: [Kfb, K1] across—30 sts.
Row 7: [K1, Kfb, K1] across—40 sts.
Row 9: [K1, Kfb, K2] across—50 sts.
Row 11: [K2, Kfb, K2] across—60 sts.
Row 13: [K2, Kfb, K3] across—70 sts.
Row 15: [K3, Kfb, K3] across—80 sts.
Row 17: [K3, Kfb, K4] across—90 sts.
Row 19: K.
Row 20: Join a strand of C. With 2 strands held tog, K for outer base edge. Cut 1 strand.
Rows 21–29: St st for outside edge.
Row 30: Rep row 20 for top edge of bowl.
Rows 31–39: St st inside edge.
Row 40: K for start of inner base edge.

INNER BASE

Rows 41–42: St st.
Row 43: [K3, K2tog, K4] across—80 sts.
Row 45: [K3, K2tog, K3] across—70 sts.
Row 47: [K2, K2tog, K3] across—60 sts.
Row 49: [K2, K2tog, K2] across—50 sts.
Row 51: [K1, K2tog, K2] across—40 sts.
Row 53: [K1, K2tog, K1] across—30 sts.
Row 55: [K1, K2tog] across—20 sts.
Row 57: K2tog across—10 sts.

Cut yarn leaving a long tail, thread tail through rem sts, gather tightly and fasten off. Sew ends of rows tog leaving inner base edge rows open. Cut a piece of cardboard to fit the base of the bowl, glue the cardboard circle to WS of base. Sew side edge rows.

BONE

With B, CO 12, pm in center st.

Rows 1–2, 6–12, 14–32, 34–40: St st.
Row 3: Kfb in each st across—24 sts.
Rows 4, 42: P.
Row 5: K4, Kfb 4 times, K8, Kfb 4 times, K4—32 sts.
Row 13: K2tog across—16 sts.
Row 33: Kfb in each st across—32 sts.
Row 41: K4, K2tog 4 times, K8, K2tog 4 times, K4—24 sts.
Row 43: K2tog across—12 sts.
Row 44: P. BO, pm at center.

Sew ends of rows tog, stuff firmly. Matching seam with center markers, whip st CO and BO edges.

FINISHING

Weave in all ends.

Samuel the Snake

Measurements

Length 42in/107cm, Height 4in/10cm

Materials

* Stylecraft Special DK 3.5oz/100g balls 100% Acrylic, one ball each:
  Citron 1263 (A), Green 1116 (B), Bottle 1009 (C), Sunshine 1114 (D),
  Matador 1010 (E), and Black 1002 (F)
* 14oz/400g Stuffing
* Knitting needles size US 2 (3mm)

Gauge

26 sts and 36 rows = 4in/10cm in St st.

UPPER BODY

With C, CO 3.

Rows 1–2, 4, 5, 7, 8: St st.
Row 3: K, inc 1 st at each end of row.
Row 6: P, inc 1 st at each end of row.
Rows 9–23: Rep rows 3–8 2 times, then rep rows 1–4—19 sts.

WORK CHART A (Rows 24–71)

Beg with Row 1 of chart, reading K rows (odd numbers) from right to left and P rows (even numbers) from left to right. Inc 1 st at each end of row 3 and every 4th row 11 times as indicated on chart. Work diamonds in intarsia method—43 sts.

KEY

- RS: knit
  WS: purl
- no stitch
- Bottle
- Green
- Matador
- Sunshine
- Red border indicates rep

CHART A

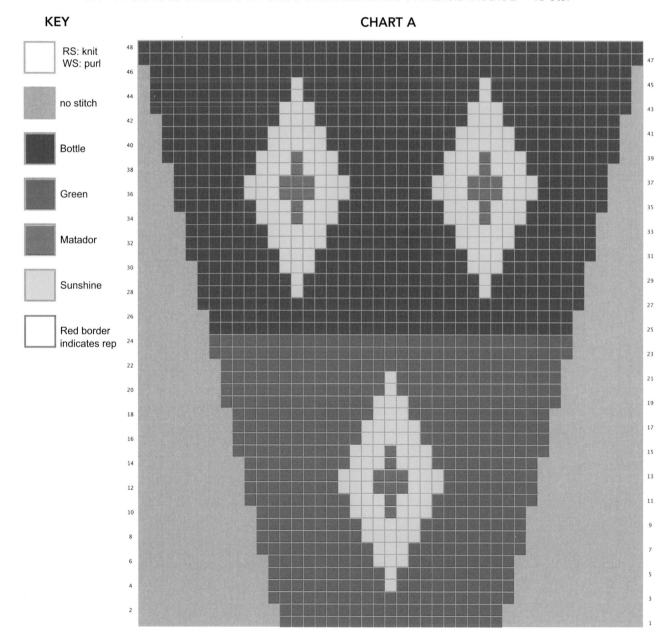

WORK CHART B (Rows 72–311): 5 times

CHART B

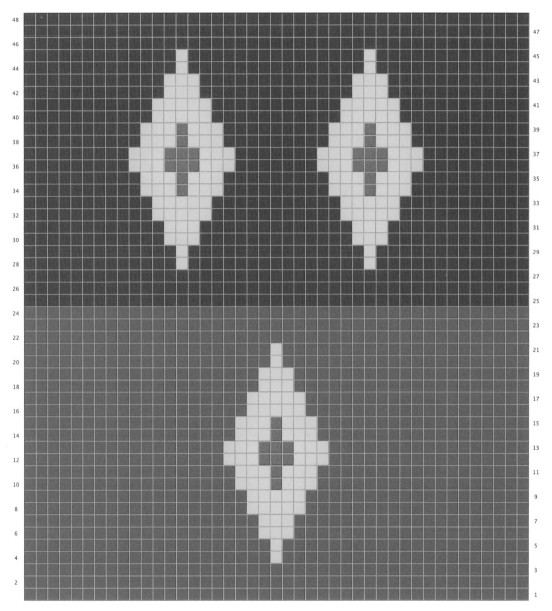

HEAD

Rows 312–315: With B, St st.
Rows 316–321: St st, CO 3 sts at beg of each row—61 sts.
Rows 322–334: St st.
Row 335: K1, [K4, K2tog, K4] across—55 sts.
Rows 336–342: St st. Pm in center st.
Row 343: K1, [K3, K2tog, K4] across—49 sts.
Rows 344–348, 350–354, 356–360, 362–364, 366–368, 370–372: St st.
Row 349: K1, [K3, K2tog, K3] across—43 sts.
Row 355: K1, [K2, K2tog, K3] across—37 sts.
Row 361: K1, [K2, K2tog, K2] across—31 sts.
Row 365: K1, [K1, K2tog, K2] across—25 sts.
Row 369: K1, [K1, K2tog, K1] across—19 sts.
Row 373: K1, [K2tog, K1] across—13 sts.
Row 374: P. BO.

UNDERBODY

With A, CO 3 sts.

Rows 1–23: Rep rows 1-23 of Upper Body—19 sts.
Row 24: St st, inc 1 st at each end of row—21 sts.
Rows 25–68: St st, inc 1 st at each end of every 4th row 11 times—43 sts.
Rows 69–311: St st.

HEAD

Rows 312–374: Rep rows 312–374 of Upper Body.

Weave in all ends. Sew upper body to underbody matching shaping, stuffing firmly before closing.

EYES (make 2)

With C, CO 5.

Row 1 and all odd number rows (WS): P.
Row 2: Kfb in each st across—10 sts.
Row 4: [Kfb, K1] across—15 sts.
Rows 6–11: With D, St st.
Row 12: [K1, K2tog] across—10 sts.
Row 14: K2tog across—5 sts.

Cut yarn leaving a long tail, thread tail through rem sts, gather tightly and fasten off. Using marker as a guide, sew row ends to head as illustrated, stuffing each eye. With F, embroider a circle of 10 chain sts in center of each eye.

NOSTRILS

With F, embroider a circle of 5 small chain sts for each nostril.

TONGUE

With E, CO 6.

Rows 1–24: St st.

Divide for end of tongue

K3, turn, working on 3 sts only, work 5 rows St st. Cut yarn leaving a long tail, thread tail through rem sts, gather tightly and fasten off. Sew row ends tog for last 5 rows only.

With RS facing, join E, work 6 rows in St st on rem 3 sts, beg with a K row. Cut yarn leaving a long tail, thread tail through rem sts, gather tightly and fasten off. Sew row ends tog. Sew CO edge to center front head seam.

FINISHING

Weave in all ends.

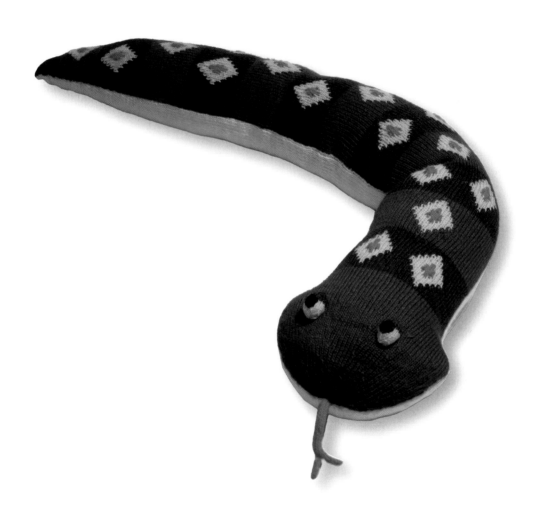

Sebastian the Starfish

Measurements
Height 12in/30cm

Materials

* Stylecraft Special DK 3.5oz/100g balls 100% Acrylic, one ball each: Jaffa 1256 (A), Black 1002 (B), White 1001 (C), and Turquoise 1068 (D)
* 2.1oz/60g Stuffing
* Stitch markers
* Knitting needles size US 2 (3mm)

Gauge
26 sts and 36 rows = 4in/10cm in St st.

BODY (make 2)

With A, CO 15 sts.

Row 1: K.
Row 2 and all WS rows: P.
Row 3: Kfb in each st across—30 sts.
Row 5: [Kfb, K1] across—45 sts.
Row 7: [K1, Kfb, K1] across—60 sts.
Rows 9, 13, 17: K.
Row 11: [K1, Kfb, K2] across—75 sts.
Row 15: [K2, Kfb, K2] across—90 sts.
Row 19: [K2, Kfb, K3] across—105 sts.
Row 20: P, pm at each end of row.

FIRST POINT

Row 21: K20, Kfb, turn. Cont working on these 22 sts only.
Rows 22–24: St st.
Row 25: St st, dec 1 st at each end of row—20 sts.

Rep the last 4 rows until 2 sts rem. Work 3 rows even in St st, BO.

REM POINTS

With RS facing, join yarn at row 20 and work as for first point.
Sew row ends from markers to center. Tightly gather CO sts and fasten off. Sew body pieces tog, matching seams, stuffing before closing.

NOSE

With A, CO 16.

Rows 1–4: St st.
Row 5: K2tog across—8 sts.

Cut yarn leaving a long tail, thread tail through rem sts, gather tightly and fasten off. Sew ends of rows tog with seam underneath nose. Stuff firmly and sew CO edge to center of body.

EYES (make 2)

With C, CO 12.

Rows 1–4: St st.
Row 5: With B, K2tog across—6 sts.

Cut yarn leaving a long tail, thread tail through rem sts, gather tightly and fasten off. Sew ends of rows tog and stuff firmly. Tightly gather CO sts and fasten off. With D, embroider a circle of 8 chain sts around B on each eye. With C, make a tiny straight stitch for the twinkle in each eye. Sew eyes 3 sts from center, 8 rows above nose.

MOUTH

With B, embroider a 'V' of two long stitches worked out from center, 4 rows below nose as illustrated.

FINISHING

Weave in all ends.

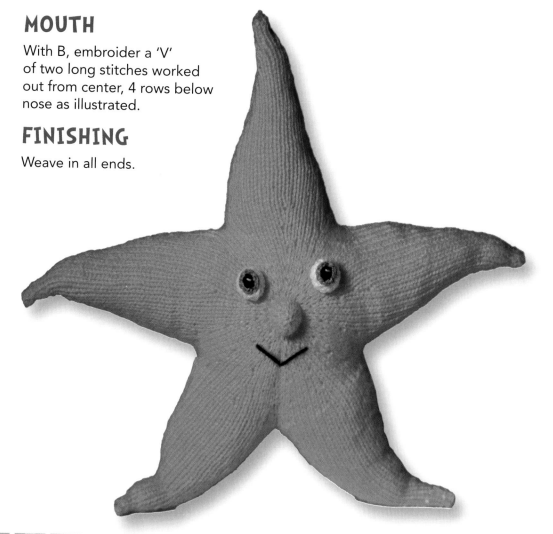

Squishy Beach Balls

Measurements

Small Ball Circumference 18in/46cm
Large Ball Circumference 36in/92cm

Materials required

* Stylecraft Special DK 3.5oz/100g balls 100% Acrylic, one ball each:
  Matador 1010 (A), Green 1116 (B), Royal 1117 (C), and Sunshine 1114 (D)

* 8.8oz/250g Stuffing

* Knitting needles size US 2 (3mm) and US 6 (4mm)

Gauge

26 sts and 36 rows = 4in/10cm in St st using US 2 (3mm) needles.
20 sts and 28 rows = 4in/10cm in St st using US 6 (4mm) needles.

NOTE: The small ball is knitted using US 2 (3mm) needles and a single strand throughout.
The large ball is knitted using US 6 (4mm) needles and two strands of yarn held together throughout.

SEGMENTS (make 2 in each color)

CO 3.

Rows 1–2, 36–64: St st.
Row 3: St st, inc 1 st at each end of row—5 sts.
Rows 4–35: St st, inc 1 st at each end of every 4th row 8 times—21 sts.
Row 65: St st, dec 1 st at each end of row—19 sts.
Rows 66–97: St st, dec 1 st at each end of every 4th row 8 times—3 sts.
Row 98: P, BO.

Sew row ends of segments tog as illustrated, stuffing firmly before closing. Tightly gather CO and BO sts and fasten off.

FINISHING

Weave in all ends.

ACKNOWLEDGMENTS

I would like to thank the following wonderful people who have helped to make this book possible: Katharine Maller for commissioning this book, Vanessa Putt for always being there when I need help or support, Kim Kotary for editing the patterns, Tommy Muller for the fantastic photography and for talking to the toys nicely so they behaved. Last but not least, the amazing team at Dover Publications.

YARN SUPPLIERS

USA
Texas Yarn Farm
Tel: (940) 923-2314
www.texasyarnfarm.com

UK
Stylecraft
P.O. Box 62
Goulbourne Street
Keighley
West Yorkshire
BD21 1PP
England
Tel: +44 (0) 153-560-9798
www.stylecraft-yarns.co.uk

ABOUT THE AUTHOR

Jody Long was born in Portsmouth, in the United Kingdom, in 1984. He grew up in Waterlooville, Hampshire, and moved to Málaga, Spain, in 2014. For over ten years, he designed for all the major U.K. and U.S. knitting magazines, then moved on to design for knitting mills around the globe. Jody has also designed for celebrity clients. His first book, *Knitted Toys*, is only the beginning of his career as an author.